REGENTS RESTORATION DRAMA SERIES

General Editor: John Loftis

THE HISTORY OF KING LEAR

NAHUM TATE

The History of King Lear

Edited by

JAMES BLACK

UNIVERSITY OF NEBRASKA PRESS • LINCOLN

Publishers on the Plains

UNP

Library of Congress Cataloging in Publication Data

Shakespeare, William, 1564–1616.
  The history of King Lear.

  (Regents Restoration drama series)
  Includes bibliographical references.
  I. Tate, Nahum, 1652–1715. II. Black, James,
1932–   ed. III. Title.
PR2878.K4T3 1975   822.3′3   74–82562
ISBN 0–8032–0382–9
ISBN 0–8032–5382–6 pbk.

MANUFACTURED IN THE UNITED STATES OF AMERICA

Regents Restoration Drama Series

The Regents Restoration Drama Series provides soundly edited texts, in modern spelling, of the more significant plays of the late seventeenth and early eighteenth centuries. The word "Restoration" is here used ambiguously and must be explained. A strict definition of the word is unacceptable to everyone, for it would exclude, among many other plays, those of Congreve. If to the historian it refers to the period between 1660 and 1685 (or 1688), it has long been used by the student of drama in default of a more precise term to refer to plays belonging to the dramatic tradition established in the 1660s, weakening after 1700, and displaced in the 1730s. It is in this extended sense—imprecise though justified by academic custom—that the word is used in this series, which includes plays first produced between 1660 and 1737. Although these limiting dates are determined by political events, the return of Charles II (and the removal of prohibitions against operation of theaters) and the passage of Walpole's Stage Licensing Act, they enclose a period of dramatic history having a coherence of its own in the establishment, development, and disintegration of a tradition.

The editors have planned the series with attention to the projected dimensions of the completed whole, a representative collection of Restoration drama providing a record of artistic achievement and providing also a record of the deepest concerns of three generations of Englishmen. And thus it contains deservedly famous plays—*The Country Wife, The Man of Mode,* and *The Way of the World*—and also significant but little known plays, *The Virtuoso,* for example, and *City Politiques,* the former a satirical review of scientific investigation in the early years of the Royal Society, the latter an equally satirical review of politics at the time of the Popish Plot. If the volumes of famous plays finally achieve the larger circulation, the other volumes may have the greater utility, in making available texts otherwise difficult of access with the editorial apparatus needed to make them intelligible.

The editors have had the instructive example of the parallel and senior project, the Regents Renaissance Drama Series; they have in fact used the editorial policies developed for the earlier plays as their own, modifying them as appropriate for the later period and as the experience of successive editions suggested. The introductions to the separate Restoration plays differ considerably in their nature. Although a uniform body of relevant information is presented in each of them, no attempt has been made to impose a pattern of interpretation. Emphasis in the introductions has necessarily varied with the nature of the plays and inevitably—we think desirably—with the special interests and aptitudes of the different editors.

Each text in the series is based on a fresh collation of the seventeenth- and eighteenth-century editions that might be presumed to have authority. The textual notes, which appear above the rule at the bottom of each page, record all substantive departures from the edition used as the copy-text. Variant substantive readings among contemporary editions are listed there as well. Editions later than the eighteenth century are referred to in the textual notes only when an emendation originating in some one of them is received into the text. Variants of accidentals (spelling, punctuation, capitalization) are not recorded in the notes except in instances in which they have, or may have, substantive relevance. Contracted forms of characters' names are silently expanded in speech prefixes and stage directions and, in the case of speech prefixes, are regularized. Additions to the stage directions of the copy-text are enclosed in brackets.

Spelling has been modernized along consciously conservative lines, but within the limits of a modernized text the linguistic quality of the original has been carefully preserved. Contracted preterites have regularly been expanded. Punctuation has been brought into accord with modern practices. The objective has been to achieve a balance between the pointing of the old editions and a system of punctuation which, without overloading the text with exclamation marks, semicolons, and dashes, will make the often loosely flowing verse and prose of the original syntactically intelligible to the modern reader. Dashes are regularly used only to indicate interrupted speeches, or shifts of address within a single speech.

Explanatory notes, chiefly concerned with glossing obsolete words and phrases, are printed below the textual notes at the bottom of each page. References to stage directions in the notes follow the admirable system of the Revels editions, whereby stage directions are keyed, decimally, to the line of the text before or after which they occur. Thus, a note on 0.2 has reference to the second line of the stage direction at the beginning of the scene in question. A note on 115.1 has reference to the first line of the stage direction following line 115 of the text of the relevant scene. Speech prefixes, and any stage directions attached to them, are keyed to the first line of accompanying dialogue.

JOHN LOFTIS

Stanford University

Contents

List of Abbreviations

Kersey	John Kersey. *Dictionarium Anglo-Britannicum, or A General English Dictionary*. London, 1708.
OED	*Oxford English Dictionary*
om.	omitted
Q1	First quarto, 1681.
Q2	Second quarto, 1689.
Q3	Third quarto, 1699.
Q4	Fourth quarto, [1702].
Q5	Fifth quarto, 1712.
S.D.	stage direction
S.P.	speech prefix
Summers	Montague Summers. *Shakespeare Adaptations*. London, 1922.

Introduction

Nahum Tate's *The History of King Lear* was entered in the Term Catalogues under May 1681. The first quarto appeared in that year "Printed for E. Flesher, and . . . sold by R. Bentley and M. Magnes in Russel-street near Covent Garden." What payment Tate received for the rights is unknown. The play went into four more printed editions during his lifetime: 1689 (Q2), 1699 (Q3), 1702 (Q4), and 1712 (Q5). All clearly extend from the first edition: the substantive reading in Q1 of III.iii.39, "beheaded" for "bareheaded," is repeated in all subsequent quartos, as are "fow storm" and "fow fiend" at III.iii.40 and 62. The first quarto's stage directions are reproduced exactly in the subsequent editions, even to the repetition of an error, "Lond. *Storm*" (III.i.45) for "*Loud Storm*." The cast-list in Q2–5 is the same as that in Q1, despite the facts that Betterton was dead by 1712 and that many of the original players had been replaced long before then. It is certain that Q2 was set from Q1; and the carrying over of a printing error from Q2's cast-list is evidence that Q3 extends from its immediate predecessor. Q3 is better punctuated than its predecessors, but omits II.ii.27–30, as does Q4; the conclusion that Q4 thus derives from Q3 is supported by the fact that each of these quartos misplaces certain lines (e.g., I.ii.29–30). Q5 has the same errors, indicating it was set from Q3 or Q4. In sum, it appears that each quarto after Q1 was set from a predecessor, and that none is more authoritative than Q1.

The copy-text for the present edition of *The History of King Lear* is a first quarto now in the Bodleian Library; a full collation of five copies of this quarto reveals no substantive or accidental variants. The other copies collated are in the British Museum, the Victoria and Albert Museum, the Birmingham Central Reference Library, and Worcester College, Oxford.

INTRODUCTION

Born and educated in Ireland, Nahum Tate had broken into London literary circles with a collection of lyric poems published in 1677, when he was twenty-five. He then tried his hand at writing plays, with *Brutus of Alba* (1678), a tragedy based on the fourth book of the *Aeneid*, and another tragedy, *The Loyal General* (1679). In 1680 he turned to adapting Shakespeare, and in a space of about eighteen months wrote versions of *King Lear*, *Richard II*, and *Coriolanus*; though *Richard II* was the first of these to be produced, the *Lear* adaptation was evidently the first to be written.[1] The idea of adapting Shakespeare was probably suggested to Tate by Dryden's alteration of *Troilus and Cressida* in 1679. Dryden appears to have been Tate's intellectual patron at this time; he contributed a prologue to *The Loyal General*, collaborated with Tate and others in *Ovid's Epistles, Translated by Several Hands* (1680), and entrusted him with writing the bulk of *The Second Part of Absalom and Achitophel* (1682).

Tate's experience in 1680 with *Richard II* was unfortunate. When the play was in production it was noticed that a seditious intent might be read into the portrayal of an English king's deposition and murder, so Tate disguised the play with a foreign setting, retitled it *The Sicilian Usurper*, and gave the characters Italianate names. In spite of this subterfuge the Lord Chamberlain banned the play after only two performances. Nor, except for *The History of King Lear*, was the rest of Tate's dramatic career particularly successful. His adaptation of *Coriolanus*, titled *The Ingratitude of a Commonwealth* (1681), an anti-Whig tract designed to show "what miseries commonwealths have been involved in by a blind compliance with their popular misleaders,"[2] was acted a few times in its first and only season.[3] He had some success with *A Duke and No Duke*, adapted in 1684 from Aston Cokain's *Trappolin Supposed a Prince*, but none with *Cuckolds-Haven* (1685; an alteration of Chapman's and Marston's *Eastward-Ho*), and *The Island Princess* (1687; adapted from Beaumont and Fletcher). His last play, *In-*

---

[1] In his dedicatory epistle to the published adaptation of *Richard II*, Tate says, "I fell upon the new-modelling of this tragedy (as I had just before done on *The History of King Lear*)."

[2] Dedicatory epistle.

[3] Tate's indication of loyalty in *The Ingratitude*, coupled with a reputation for piety and, perhaps, poetical accomplishment, may have influenced his appointment as Laureate in 1692.

jured Love (1707), another adaptation, this time from Webster's *The White Devil*, was "designed to be acted at the Theatre Royal," but was never produced. Aside from *The History of King Lear*, Tate's only remembered work for the theater is his libretto for Purcell's *Dido and Aeneas* (1689).

In spite of Dryden's observation (made in another context) that "to copy the best author is a kind of praise," more scorn than commendation has been Tate's return for adapting Shakespeare's great tragedy. *The History of King Lear* may claim to be one of the most famous unread plays in English; it is unique in having attracted a special kind of word-of-mouth ridicule, with the result that "the *King Lear* with the happy ending" has long had far more critics than readers. It is almost idle to cite the printed scorn that the play has attracted, from Addison's statement that in adaptation *King Lear* had "lost half its beauty," through Charles Lamb's protest that Tate "had put his hook in the nostrils of this Leviathan for . . . the showmen of the scene to draw the mighty beast about more easily," down to Hazelton Spencer's contemptuous dismissal of it in this century as a "hodge-podge." Even Maynard Mack, evaluating the adaptation for the light it throws on the original, says that Tate's *Lear* "invites ridicule and deserves it."[4]

But Tate's version, or aspects of it, has also had its defenders, from Johnson's approval of the happy ending to recent thoughtful evaluations of the text by Christopher Spencer and W. Moelwyn Merchant.[5] And the fact that the play was a great popular success cannot be ignored; part of Tate's "offense" is that his version, and revisions of it, kept Shakespeare's from the stage for a century and a half.

[4]Addison, *Spectator,* no. 40; Lamb, "On the Tragedies of Shakespeare," in *Works*, ed. E. V. Lucas (London, 1903), 1:107; Spencer, *Shakespeare Improved* (Cambridge, Mass., 1927), p. 251; Mack, *King Lear in Our Time* (Berkeley, 1965), p. 9.

[5]*Johnson on Shakespeare*, ed. Walter Raleigh (Oxford, 1908), pp. 161–62; Spencer, "A Word for Tate's *Lear*," *Studies in English Literature* 3 (Spring 1963): 241–52. See also Spencer's introduction to *Five Restoration Adaptations of Shakespeare* (Urbana, Ill., 1965), and his *Nahum Tate* (New York, 1972), pp. 67–75. Merchant's discussion of the *History* is in "Shakespeare 'Made Fit,' " in *Restoration Theatre*, Stratford-upon-Avon Studies 6 (New York, 1965), Chap. 9.

Obviously Tate did not undertake the adaptation (hereafter referred to as the *History*) out of a lack of respect for Shakespeare's work. He was a learned dramatic theorist, as can be seen from the great wealth of classical and modern citations in the essay on farce which is his preface to the second edition (1693) of *A Duke and No Duke*; he held Shakespeare in great esteem, and discussed his art in *The Loyal General*'s dedicatory epistle, where he argues with reference to *3 Henry VI* and *Richard III* that Shakespeare always observed decorum of characterization and concludes that his learning must have been "more than common report allows him." Tate's Prologue and Epilogue to the *History* also reflect this respectful attitude toward Shakespeare. But *King Lear* was not a play that recommended itself to Restoration audiences.[6] The reasons for the popular success of Tate's version lie in his transformation of Shakespeare's play into typical Restoration drama.

Before dealing with the ways in which Tate effected that transformation, however, one may well ask why he chose *Lear* for adaptation. The answer would seem to lie in the relationship between Tate's earlier play, *The Loyal General*, and Shakespeare's *Lear*. The plot parallels between the two plays are striking. *The Loyal General* is about an old and irascible king who is tired of ruling. Surrounded by people—including his young wife and her former lover—who are scheming to acquire his power and who mislead him with lies and forged letters, he also has a deeply loyal and affectionate daughter, Arviola. The kingdom falls into disorder and the king's loyal general, one Theocrin, is betrayed and disgraced. There follows much wandering on a moor during a storm, and a final cataclysm in which Arviola stabs herself to death and Theocrin swallows poison which causes him to rave misogynistically before he dies.

One might easily conclude that Tate borrowed some of the incidents from Shakespeare, and that he used Shakespeare's Lear and Cordelia as models for his king and Arviola. But he implies in

[6]Only two or three performances of Shakespeare's *Lear* are known between the Restoration and the staging of the *History* (see my article "An Augustan Stage-History: Nahum Tate's *King Lear*," *Restoration and Eighteenth-Century Theatre Research* 6 [May 1967]: 36–54, especially p. 36). Tate suggests in the dedication that when he came to *Lear* it was new to him, although *Lear* was performed in London on 29 June 1675.

the dedicatory epistle to the *History* that he had not read Shakespeare's version until Thomas Boteler, to whom he dedicated the play, recommended it to him: "I found the whole to answer your account of it. . . ." That implication is strongly supported by the fact that although *The Loyal General* contains frequent verbal echoes of Shakespeare, none of them are from *Lear*; Tate is such a derivative dramatist that if he had been borrowing plot one would expect him to have borrowed lines and phrases as well. It seems most likely, therefore, that Boteler's awareness of the similarities between *Lear* and *The Loyal General* prompted him to propose to Tate that he attempt "the revival of *Lear* with alterations," perhaps suggesting that in view of the resemblances Tate would find it no very hard task to adapt the play.

Tate made the task even easier by reusing incidents and lines from *The Loyal General*; though his usual method of proceeding was to eke out his own imagination with the products of others', in the *History* he borrows from himself. Aside from its fatal ending, the love story of Arviola and her general corresponds to that of the *History*'s Edgar and Cordelia. In fact that correspondence very likely explains how, at least at the surface level, Tate lighted upon his "one expedient to rectify what was wanting in the regularity and probability of the tale"—the love story: he simply made Edgar and Cordelia the counterparts of the lovers in the earlier play. One of their dramatic adventures derives from *The Loyal General*. A high point of that play is Arviola's rescue from would-be rapists (V.vi); a similar incident is used in the *History*, III.iv, where lines 73 to 79 are transcribed straight from the earlier play.

In making these changes in *Lear*, Tate was influenced of course not only by his earlier play but also by the demands of his audience. He says he found Shakespeare's play "a heap of jewels, unstrung and unpolished . . . dazzling in their disorder," and undertook a work of stringing. He did not do so aimlessly: his scenes are disposed in a manner that gives his play a great deal of variety and many changes of pace. The contemporary demand was for good theater, rather than good drama, and Tate's *History of King Lear* is excellent theater.

What did Restoration audiences expect from a play? For one thing—action. Violent and rapid activity had made Nathaniel Lee's plays successful; as one of Lee's contemporaries put it:

The more constant and violent the action is, the more it will be attended by audiences. Wherever there is passion, there must necessarily be action. . . . It is this quality that has preserved and still keeps up *Alexander the Great*, which Mr. Crowne found fault with . . . because it was continually on the fret, as he called it . . . ; that is, the passions were lively and strong enough through the whole piece, which so took up the audience, that they had no leisure or interval to grow weary and be disgusted.[7]

In *Of Dramatic Poesy* the crowning compliment paid to Jonson's *The Silent Woman* is that "the business of it rises in every act."[8] Shakespeare's play is not, of course, short on action; but to the storm, blinding, battle, and duel Tate adds an attempted rape, the preliminaries to hanging, and Lear's fight and rescue in prison—all of these additions being worked in coherently, if not always consistently with the spirit of the original. For example, in both the original and the adaptation Lear exclaims, "Let copulation thrive!" but there is no indication that to Tate the attempted rape of Cordelia has anything to do with a state of moral anarchy following on Lear's relinquishment of power. A rape, or an attempt at it, was almost an essential feature of a Restoration play. So conventional is this that John Dennis might be referring to the *History* when he grumbles that "a rape is the peculiar barbarity of our English stage . . . . In tragedy it is a panegyric upon the female sex."[9]

Restoration playgoers also expected a love interest; they had, after all, dieted on heroic plays for at least fifteen years and were familiar with the dilemma of the play's distressed lovers, caught in the conflict between love and duty and exhibiting heroic virtue in the face of trials. The exhibition of love had been recommended by some of the most weighty critics, as a means of tempering

[7]*Miscellanea Aurea*, attributed to Thomas Killigrew (London, 1720), pp. 37–38: quoted in R. G. Ham, *Otway and Lee* (New Haven, 1931), p. 74.

[8]John Dryden, *"Of Dramatic Poesy" and Other Critical Essays*, ed. George Watson, 2 vols. (London and New York, 1967), 1:75. All subsequent references to Dryden's criticism cite this edition as "Watson."

[9]*Original Letters* (London, 1721), p. 63. Stage rape is a panegyric upon females, says Dennis, because "there the woman has all the advantage of the man. For she is supposed to remain innocent, and to be pleas'd without her consent; while the man, who is accounted a damned villain, proclaims the power of female charms, which have the force to drive him to so horrid a violence."

"those black ideas which the ancient tragedy caused in us by superstition and terror."[10] In *Of Dramatic Poesy* Eugenius says:

> For love-scenes, you will find few among [the ancient tragedies], whose gentleness would have tempered them, which is the most frequent of all the passions.[11]

Tate takes treble advantage: he gives Edgar a respectable passion for Cordelia, contrasts it with Edmund's aggressive lust, and also expands with sensational detail the Shakespearean love-triangle between Edmund and the wicked daughters.

It is not unfair to Tate, or to any Restoration dramatist, to break down his play in this manner into a list of components or features. Asked to describe Tate's *Lear*, a contemporary playgoer probably would have ticked off a rejection scene, a storm scene, scenes of love-making, fighting, and so on. Christopher Spencer, for example, says that "doubtless Tate's contemporaries . . . were attracted to the theater less by the consistency or quality of style than by adequately written scenes of the kinds they liked to see, hung together on an interesting story line."[12]

Another expectation of Restoration audiences was that a tragedy would be uniformly serious. It is true that in 1680 Dryden had written the tragicomic *Spanish Friar* in the belief that audiences had "grown weary of continued melancholy scenes."[13] His *Don Sebastian* (1689) and Otway's *Venice Preserved* (1682) also have comic episodes. But Tate was not an innovator: what he saw as a requirement of uniform seriousness led to the excision of Shakespeare's Fool. Tate obviously had no conception of the kind of comic business that complements and furthers a tragic plot in the way that the Fool's actions and speeches do in *King Lear*. And even if he had realized that Shakespeare's Fool is essentially a tragic rather than a comic figure, Augustan decorum of characterization held with Dryden that "no man is at leisure to make

[10]E. Saint-Évremond, *De la Tragédie ancienne et moderne*, 1672, trans. Pierre des Maizeaux (London, 1714), 2:22.

[11]Watson, 1:41–42.

[12]"A Word for Tate's *Lear*," p. 250.

[13]Epistle Dedicatory, Watson, 1:279. Perhaps with an eye on Dryden's experiments, Tate ineptly mingled comedy and tragedy in his versions of *Richard II* and *Coriolanus*. It might be argued that the Restoration fop in the *History*, Tate's version of Shakespeare's Oswald, is a figure more ridiculous and less menacing than his original.

sentences and similes when his soul is in an agony."[14] Restoration audiences would have recognized the Fool only as some sort of Harlequin; in an age when the "action" of a play was especially stressed, they would have asked, Just what does the Fool *do*? In Shakespeare's play he is Lear's conscience, and fosters his master's realization of error and folly. But in Tate's version Lear is not guilty to the extent that he is in Shakespeare; neither is there a gradual apprehension on his part that his daughters have misled him. Since Tate's play races swiftly to the outbursts against Gonerill and Regan without Lear's noticing "a most faint neglect of late," and without his growing conception of error—"I did her wrong"—the Fool would have no function. Tate has excised the part cleanly, except for one detail. In the original the Fool is the object of the king's pity as Lear comes to realize that others are suffering in the storm. Tate has retained the expression of pity, which Lear now addresses, somewhat incongruously, to Kent (III.i.41–46).

Though none of the other Shakespearean characters have been eliminated, they have all been affected by the requirements of Restoration audiences. Tate saw that Shakespeare's hero could baffle such an audience, particularly by his motives and conduct in the first act. Attempting to make the king more understandable or at least more recognizable, he prepares for Lear's irrational behavior by introducing "choler" as a tragic flaw[15]—picking up from the original Goneril's insinuation about her father's "infirm and choleric years." In Tate, it is Edmund, working on Lear's choler, who sparks off the train of events; Edmund appears at the start of the play to announce that he already has poisoned Gloster's mind against Edgar, and it soon is apparent that the poison has reached Lear as well (I.i.118–21). (Having Lear misled by Edmund as well as by the elder daughters also serves to unify the main plot and subplot.) Thus the audience is helped to place Lear—that is, to fit him into a stage category such as choleric king, deluded ruler or even, as Christopher Spencer suggests, typical bewildered parent.[16]

It seems possible that another aspect of the character of Tate's Lear, his desire for retirement, is a reflection of Tate's own

[14]*The Grounds of Criticism in Tragedy*, Watson, 1:256.
[15]See I.i.54–55, 93, 117.
[16]"A Word for Tate's *Lear*," p. 245.

character. The king in his *Loyal General* is also seeking retirement; and Tate's lyric poetry often expresses such a desire, which is manifested in pastoral yearnings and morbid thoughts about death.[17] Though *King Lear*, as Tate found it, could have had a good deal to say to Restoration audiences about the dangers of power carelessly delegated,[18] Tate had neither the temperament nor the inclination to attempt a reshaping of the Shakespearean theme of responsibility. His Lear wants to retire, and gets his wish in the end, having learned nothing and forgotten nothing:

> Thou, Kent and I, retired to some cool cell,
> Will gently pass our short reserves of time
> In calm reflections on our fortunes past.

The speech, "Come, let's away to prison . . . ," as adapted and delivered in Tate's context, thus has become a kind of hymn to retirement; prison is a sanctuary from the world. This is not the chastened and wiser Shakespearean Lear, determining with his new knowledge to make the best even of prison, but still the hero of Tate's first act, rather vacantly happy to be rid of the "toil of state." Yet Tate's sense of theater is still active; he gives the speech a good deal of irony by making Gonerill plan her father's death just before it.

Cordelia and Edgar, like Lear, have become figures recognizable to their audience. In Tate, Cordelia has lost her enigmatic quality and become the typical Restoration heroine of unqualified virtue, caught up in not one but two heroic-play dilemmas. As mentioned above, the first of these is love versus duty: whether to marry Burgundy, her father's choice, or to keep herself unattached for Edgar. Her second dilemma is whether, after seeing an example of male self-seeking in Burgundy, she should entrust herself to Edgar. Basically, Cordelia is recognizable to the audience as beautiful, in love, and in difficulty. Edgar is her male

[17]H. F. Scott-Thomas detects in Tate's verse "nausea at the conventions and chicanery of Court life, and his longing for the . . . country" ("Nahum Tate and the Seventeenth Century," *English Literary History* 1 [1934]: 270). A poem where these inclinations are especially prominent is "The Choice" in the 1677 collection.

[18]Hobbes had said that the first element which tends toward the dissolution of a commonwealth is "want of absolute power" in the ruler (*Leviathan*, Part 2, chap. 29); and Dryden makes this point dramatically in *The Indian Emperor* (1665): "Kings and their crowns have but one destiny: Power is their life; when that expires, they die" (V.ii.226–27).

counterpart, and little more need be done in characterizing them: they are what Dryden calls "examples of moral virtue writ in verse."[19]

However, Tate's literary consciousness has affected his portrayal of these two characters. His interest in epic—an interest which is reflected in a discussion of the respective merits of epic and tragedy in *The Loyal General*'s prefatory epistle—leads to the tagging of Edgar and Cordelia as "pious." In only one of the eight instances of its use in Tate's *Lear* does the word "piety" mean religious devotion. Like Virgil when he characterized his hero as *pius Aeneas*, Tate generally means by piety the dutiful regard and affection of men and women for those who have a natural claim upon them.[20] In *The Grounds of Criticism in Tragedy* (1679) Dryden had written that "When Virgil had once given the name of *pious* to Aeneas, he was bound to show him such, in all his words and actions, through the whole poem";[21] Aeneas is especially "pious" because of his care of the Penates, and for having carried his father from the flames of Troy.[22] Tate's Edgar and Cordelia are modelled to exactly this pattern; they show proper respect for "the gods" and deliver their parents from adversity. Cordelia is a "pious princess" (IV.ii.91); she is said to have piety enough to atone for her sisters' crimes (III.ii.90–91); and Lear, finally reconciled to her, pleads for the life of his "true pious daughter" (V.vi.32). By contrast, Gonerill and Regan are the "impious sisters" (III.ii.99). The classical force of the epithet is emphasized in the play's final scene (V.vi.111), when Albany greets Edgar and Gloster:

> Look, sir, where pious Edgar comes
> Leading his eyeless father.[23]

The entrance of father and son is a set-piece, designed to fill the hiatus left by the exclusion of "Re-enter Lear, with Cordelia dead

[19]*Of Heroic Plays*, Watson, 1:157–58.

[20]It is useful here to recall that Tate's first play, *Brutus of Alba*, was a dramatization of Book 4 of the *Aeneid*. In addition to the uses of the word "piety" I have cited, see also II.v.101, V.vi.124, and (with the exceptional connotation) IV.v.66.

[21]Watson, 1:249.

[22]See T. E. Page, ed., *Virgil's Aeneid* (London, 1951), 1:100.

[23]A line or two further on Gloster refers to Edgar as "My pious son, more dear than my lost eyes."

in his arms." Tate apparently recognized the greatness of this Shakespearean entrance: to compensate for its excision he offers one of the best things he knows, a reminiscence of Aeneas bringing Anchises out of Troy.

Gloster becomes in the *History* merely another of the "good" people. Tate has removed the flippancy which Shakespeare gave the character; instead of bragging, as in Shakespeare, that he puts up with Edmund because "there was good sport at his making," Gloster explains the Bastard as "the wild sally of my youth." Gloster is another edition of at least one aspect of Lear, an irascible and abused parent who comes to know the truth. The fact that he is portrayed as at least Lear's equal in suffering shows Tate's failure to grasp an essential point about Shakespeare's play and hero, which is that Lear is the greatest sufferer of all.[24]

Tate's evil characters—Gonerill, Regan, and Edmund—seem less real than their Shakespearean counterparts; their program of villainy is greater and their blood if anything colder. While all of the "good" characters act spontaneously and impulsively, the villainous characters move with deliberation: they write and forge letters, have "projects," plan rape and murder, and consider the most appropriate time to administer poison. They revel at a masque while the good characters endure the storm; Regan dallies with Edmund while her husband is dying, compounding the evil by wishing that he would die quickly.

To the character of Edmund, however, Tate added another dimension: Edmund is another typical Restoration character, a "natural man." Based upon widespread misinterpretation of Hobbes's propositions concerning "liberty" and the "state of nature," a stereotyped idea of the natural man had grown up in the Restoration era; read out of context, certain passages of *Leviathan* were thought to be a program for libertinism.[25] This popular

[24]In Shakespeare, Lear's sufferings are comprehensive. His mental darkness is at least the counterpart of Gloucester's physical blindness; Gloster has the chance to "bear free and patient thoughts," a chance denied to the mad king. Edgar's speech beginning "When we see our betters bearing our woes" (III.vi.105–13) is a reminder that Lear is enduring Edgar's pain and more. This speech has been cut in adaptation.

[25]This belief was reinforced by popular accounts of the career of John Wilmot, Earl of Rochester, who professed to be a Hobbist and who was reported to have said on his deathbed that Hobbes's "absurd and foolish philosophy" had undone him (Robert Parsons, *A Sermon Preached at the Funeral of the Right Honorable John Earl of Rochester* [Oxford, 1680], p. 26).

belief had been translated into impressive theatrical terms in Settle's Crimalhaz (*The Empress of Morocco*, 1673), Dryden's Zempoalla (*The Indian Queen*, 1663), Maximin (*Tyrannic Love*, 1669), and Morat (*Aureng-Zebe*, 1675) and Otway's Don John (*Don Carlos*, 1675). All of these characters disregard morality and worship success, as does Tate's Edmund, who in his love of pleasure, in his total self-interest (I.i.297–98), and in his identification of himself as a libertine (V.v.19–20) is a "Hobbesian" man; indeed, he often echoes phrases from *Leviathan*.[26] Edmund is the figure of greatest literary interest in the adaptation. He tends to speak with something of the catchy vigor of Cibber's famous additions to *Richard III* ("Off with his head. So much for Buckingham"), as for example in his admission of defeat: "Legitimacy/ At last has got it." In this as in his other reworkings of Shakespeare's characterizations Tate knew what would catch the fancy of a contemporary audience.

Many of his other additions and alterations demonstrate his knowledge of his audience and his sense of theater. The confrontation of Gonerill and Regan over the dying Edmund (V.v) is the kind of scene that was popular with both audiences and playwrights.[27] As indicated by the ironical opening to his Prologue, "Since by mistakes your best delights are made," Tate also knew that mistaken identity and disguise were still acceptable theatrical devices in 1680:[28] to the disguised persons of the original (Edgar in several changes, and Kent), he added a disguised Cordelia in Act III, and he exploits the possibilities of mistaken identity when Cordelia and Edgar meet on the heath.

[26]For a fuller discussion of Edmund's Hobbism see my article "The Influence of Hobbes on Nahum Tate's *King Lear*," *Studies in English Literature* 7 (Summer 1967), 377–85.

[27]Dryden's manoeuvering Cleopatra and Octavia together in *All for Love* is probably the archetype. In any case Tate had to provide opportunities for the female members of the company which produced his play. The Duke's Theatre, for about a year before and after 1680, had no less than seven very capable actresses on its books. They were Elizabeth Barry (Cordelia), Mary Lee (Regan), Ann Shadwell (Gonerill), Elinor Leigh, Anne Marshall, Mrs. Norris, and Elizabeth Currer. See John H. Wilson, *All the King's Ladies* (Chicago, 1958), p. 104. Tate could well be lavish in his enlargement of the parts of Gonerill and Regan.

[28]For example, in September 1679 Aphra Behn's *The Young King; or The Mistake*, a play replete with such devices, had opened at the Duke's.

Another theatrical device is the "answering quality" of his scenes and actions. The logic of his plot—wherein Edgar, who succors the father who had wronged him, marries the girl who had aided the father who had wronged her[29]—is reflected in the manner whereby certain scenes correspond to one another. Cordelia praying in IV.v is a reminiscence of Lear praying in III.iii; in V.vi Edgar comes on, once more leading Gloster, and the latter, who has already knelt before Lear (IV.iv.112) with "Let me kiss that hand," does so again: "O let me kiss that once more sceptered hand." Tate also makes effective use of the "discovered" tableaux—Edmund and Regan in the grotto at the opening of IV.i, Lear with Cordelia in IV.v, and the prison tableau which opens the final scene. Even one of Tate's harshest critics in the eighteenth century, Thomas Davies, was impressed by the prison tableau:

> It must be confessed, that in the conduct of some scenes . . . Tate is not unhappy. One situation of his is particularly affecting: where the scene opens, and discovers Lear with his head on Cordelia's lap, and the king, in his sleep, attacking the forces of his enemies.[30]

Tate seems to have had few doubts about the probable success of such alterations of plot and characterization; but he appears not to have been so certain about the effect of the altered conclusion of the play. He confesses in his Dedication that after making the *History* "conclude in a success to the innocent distressed persons" he was "racked with no small fears for so bold a change, 'til [he] found it well received by [the] audience." Even with this success in the theater behind him, he feels it necessary to justify his happy ending with a quotation from Dryden in the Dedication, where he also says that it was the love plot which "necessarily" caused him to conclude the play happily—implying that the notorious happy ending came about simply because one thing led to another. But Tate was so diffident that often he can be found claiming outside persuasion or compulsion to do one thing or another where a more confident author would say that he took a

---

[29]This is Kenneth Muir's description of the action of Tate's *Lear*, which Muir says has "a certain crude logic" ("Three Shakespearean Adaptations," *Proc. of the Leeds Phil. and Lit. Soc.* 7 [1959]: 238). A Restoration audience would not have considered the logic of the action crude.

[30]*Dramatic Miscellanies* (London, 1783), 2:326.

certain decision to satisfy himself. Each of his first two plays has a love plot, and neither ends happily: the lovers in *The Loyal General* are as innocent and distressed as Edgar and Cordelia, yet they perish spectacularly. Why then the happy ending for the *History*?

It seems likely that Tate, like other of *Lear*'s readers, found the tragic ending too painful; recognizing the balance of Shakespeare's play just at the point where Albany exclaims, "Run, run! O run!" he decided, for once, to tip the scales in favor of felicity. He makes the rescuers arrive in time, and with bustle enough to smother scepticism. H. B. Charlton has shrewdly observed that Tate was mainly interested in saving Cordelia and thus missed the point of Shakespeare's tragedy.[31] In the exemplary victory of Edgar and Cordelia lies of course the philosophic difference between Shakespeare's *King Lear* and Tate's alteration. Edgar's concluding lines to "divine Cordelia"—

> Thy bright example shall convince the world
> (Whatever storms of fortune are decreed)
> That truth and virtue shall at last succeed—

are a world of experience removed from

> The weight of this sad time we must obey,
> Speak what we feel, not what we ought to say:
> The oldest hath borne most, we that are young,
> Shall never see so much, nor live so long.

But it is pointless to require from Tate what only Shakespeare had to give. Tate evidently felt that his audience was ready for the happy ending, and according to his own testimony he guessed correctly.

Eighteenth-century critics repeatedly endorsed Tate's ending. It would be easy to dismiss the opinions of the journalists in reviews of performances, for such opinions might well have been influenced by good acting. But even critics who knew both Shakespeare's and Tate's plays had good things to say about the happy ending. Charles Gildon, writing in no less a place than Rowe's 1710 edition of Shakespeare, says that "the King and Cordelia ought by no means to have dy'd, and therefore Mr. Tate has very justly altered that particular, which must disgust the reader and audience to have virtue and piety meet so unjust a reward."

[31]*Shakespearean Tragedy* (Cambridge, 1961), p. 228.

Lewis Theobald asserted in 1715 that Cordelia and Lear "ought to have survived, as Mr. Tate has made them in his alteration . . . . Virtue ought to be rewarded, as well as vice punished, but in their deaths this moral is broke through." [32] In 1754 Arthur Murphy expressed the opinion that "the play, as it is altered, will always be most agreeable to an audience." [33]

Many of the remarks dealt with the concept of poetic justice. Addison, in *The Spectator*, no. 40 (1711), criticized Tate for purveying the "chimerical notion of poetical justice" (though it should be remembered that the weight of his criticism fell mainly upon the notion, not just the play, for Addison was at the time intent upon discrediting the concept of poetic justice in order to influence the public's reception of *Cato*).[34] Generally, poetic justice was held to consist more in punishment of evil-doers than in rewarding the virtuous. Thomas Rymer usually stresses the punitive aspect,[35] and so does Dryden, as in the Preface to *An Evening's Love* (1671):

> In tragedy, where the actions and persons are great, and the crimes horrid, the laws of justice are more strictly to be observed, and examples of punishment to be made to deter mankind from the pursuit of vice.[36]

In both Shakespeare and Tate, evil is punished, though Tate makes two of his villains' punishment more "poetic" in one respect: his Gonerill and Regan kill one another, "each by the other poisoned at a banquet."

But there was a recognized place on the Augustan literary scene for plays where virtue was rewarded as well as villainy punished—a place for "tragedies" with happy endings. (It is worth noticing that although Tate changed the title of the play to *The History of King Lear*, the head-title in all the quartos reads *King Lear, a Tragedy*.) Dryden discusses the usefulness of such plays in *Heads of an Answer to Rymer* (1677), where he argues that tragedies

[32] *The Censor*, no. 10 (2 May 1715).

[33] *Gray's Inn Journal*, 19 January 1754.

[34] "Dennis has remarked," says Johnson in his commentary on Shakespeare's *King Lear* (*Johnson on Shakespeare*, p. 161), "that, to secure the favorable reception of *Cato*, the town was poisoned with much false and abominable criticism."

[35] See Rymer's *Works*, ed. Curt A. Zimansky, pp. 27–28.

[36] Watson, 1:151.

which raise joy "by showing a wicked man punished, or a good man at last fortunate are as necessary as those which raise terror and pity." He adds, however, that Aristotle "places tragedies of this kind in the second form";[37] and in *The Grounds of Criticism in Tragedy* (1679), he speaks of those "inferior sort of tragedies which end with a prosperous event." [38] Rymer says that such plays usually were unsuccessful, though he may be biased: his observation appears in the Advertisement to his tragedy *Edgar* (1677), which he claims failed in the theater because it ended "prosperously; a sort of tragedy which rarely succeeds; men being apter to pity the distressed than to rejoice with the prosperous."

Obviously that was not true of the *History*. But why should Tate, after ending *Lear* happily, congratulate himself in the dedicatory epistle upon having increased the "distress" of the plot?

> 'Twas my good fortune to light on one expedient to rectify what was wanting in the regularity and probability of the tale . . . a love betwixt Edgar and Cordelia . . . . The distress of the story is evidently heightened by it.

This is not so grotesque as it may seem. "Distress" was Tate's term for one of the "passions," and all of the disputants in Dryden's *Of Dramatic Poesy* (1668) acknowledge that representation of the passions was to be the poet's concern. Basically the passions were pity, fear, and terror; but in tragic practice terror had become only one of the emotions to be aroused in what Saint-Évremond calls "an agreeable uneasiness" or "distress," and what Dryden terms "a pleasing admiration and concernment."[39] The playwrights of the Restoration were less interested in the spiritual value of Aristotelean terror than in collecting the small change of "agreeable uneasiness," the quick returns of which accrued to the playgoer. These returns were the sense of benevolence he experienced when he pitied virtue in distress, and his sense of security arising from the spectacle of virtue triumphant and vice punished. Though of little weight by Aristotelean and Shakespearean standards, Tate's "distress" was current emotional coin at the time. In contemporary terms—that is, by the standard that

[37]Ibid., 1:217–18.

[38]Ibid., 1:247.

[39]Saint-Évremond, *De la Tragédie ancienne et moderne*, 2:18; Dryden, *Of Dramatic Poesy*, Watson, 1:218.

"the passions represented [must be] conformable to the thoughts of the audience"[40]—"distress" must be allowed some recognition.

The change in taste indicated by this reinterpretation of terror had been developing for about a hundred years; Castelvetro in sixteenth-century Italy as well as Hedelin, Saint-Évremond, and Dryden in seventeenth-century France and England can be found questioning whether audiences were not brutalized more than elevated by tragic spectacles.[41] Audiences, made callous either by over-exposure to stage carnage or by prevailing social cynicism, tended to laugh when they were supposed to be appalled. In *Of Dramatic Poesy* Lisideius says, "I have observed that in all our tragedies, the audience cannot forbear laughing when the actors are to die; it is the most comic part of the whole play."[42] Tate says in his dedicatory epistle to the *History* that the encumbering of a stage with dead bodies "makes many tragedies conclude with un-seasonable jests."

The idea of pity, like the idea of terror, also was changing. The Restoration did not regard pity as an emotion of which or through which audiences were to be purged; rather it was a highly creditable feeling, a sign of humanity and even of breeding. Hobbes had defined pity as "imagination or fiction of future calamity to ourselves, proceeding from the sense of another man's calamity,"[43] but by the last quarter of the seventeenth century, if not before, pity was being regarded as arising out of a more social instinct than self-love. Dryden preferred to think of it in "a larger sense," as "a concernment for the good."[44]

In the devaluation of terror and revaluation of pity are the impulses to stage sentimentalism. With the older tragic values in fluctuating esteem the exact definitions of pity, fear, or "distress" lay open to individual interpretation, and the poet of the later 1600s was free to mix dramatic emotion to his own recipe. Thus

[40]Dryden, *Heads of an Answer to Rymer*, Watson, 1:216.

[41]Castelvetro's discussion is in *The Poetics of Aristotle Translated and Annotated*, 1571 (in A. H. Gilbert, ed., *Literary Criticism, Plato to Dryden* [New York, 1940]; see esp. p. 349); Hedelin's in *La Pratique du théatre*, 1657 (Englished in 1684 as *The Whole Art of the Stage*); Saint-Évremond's in *De la Tragédie ancienne et moderne*, see esp. 2:21).

[42]Watson, 1:51.

[43]*Of Human Nature*, in *The English Works*, ed. W. Molesworth, 4:44.

[44]*Heads of an Answer to Rymer*, Watson 1:213.

we can see Tate's own emotional inclinations asserting themselves to "heighten" the feeling of *King Lear*. Written sixteen years before Cibber's *Love's Last Shift*, the *History* is in many ways a sentimental play. As Arthur Sherbo has outlined them, the sentimental ingredients are: a strong moral tendency; greater appeal to the emotions than to the intellect; the placing of the characters in exaggerated or artificial situations; emphasis upon the perfectibility of human nature and upon pity, with tears solicited for the sufferings of the good and admiration for their virtue; and deliberate prolongation of pathetic scenes.[45] Even a cursory reading of Tate's adaptation will confirm that it has as much affinity with the later sentimental drama as with heroic tragedy.

The sentimental strain in the *History* is perhaps most noticeable in Tate's frequent prolongation of scenes or speeches in order to wring from them the last drop of pathos. An example is in V.iv, where Lear, Cordelia, and Kent are committed to prison. In Shakespeare (V.iii) Lear and Cordelia appear as prisoners only for the brief time taken to play out the poignant but dignified scene in which Lear resolves to bear prison contentedly with his daughter—just twenty-five lines in all. In Tate's version they are in full view, from their entrance until they begin to speak, during the time needed to play a forty-four line passage. For this length of time the audience sees the mournful spectacle of Lear, at least, in chains (l. 49), and Gonerill plotting against her father while he stands nearby. Then when the three prisoners are left with their guards the scene is prolonged while Lear commiserates with Kent and weeps for "Cajus," swoons from the shock of Kent's revealing himself as the servant, and finally delivers a version of "Come, let's away to prison . . ." in which the original's "We two alone will sing, like birds i' the cage" has become a pathetic vignette: "We two will sit alone, like birds i' the cage." As they are led away, a final touch of almost triumphant pathos is Lear's anticipation of death:

> Together we'll out-toil the spite of hell
> And die the wonders of the world.

In Tate's III.iv there is an excellent example of another prolongation device, the sentimentalist's technique of arousing emo-

---

[45]Sherbo, *English Sentimental Drama* (Ann Arbor, 1957), p. 13.

tion through "allowing the spectator or one . . . of the characters
. . . to know of some impending piece of good news and [keeping
the news] from the character . . . whose distress will be relieved by
it, by doling it out a little at a time." Sherbo, whose explanation
this is,[46] calls the technique "indulging . . . in emotion for
emotion's sake." In withholding Edgar's identity from Cordelia
for the space of thirty-six lines (ll. 21–57) and making Edgar keep
up his disguise while debating whether to reveal himself, Tate is
clearly working upon his audience's feelings. An even more striking example of his use of this technique is afforded by V.vi, which
is a scene of considerable artifice. After Lear and Cordelia have
been rescued by Albany and Edgar it remains, before the happy
ending can be consummated, to convince Lear that his troubles
really are over. Thus there is a passage which exactly reflects and
reverses the movement of II.v. In the earlier scene, Lear, determined to overlook his daughters' cruelties and to think well of
them, is forced gradually into a realization of their malevolence.
In V.vi, determinedly sceptical this time, he is slowly brought to
see that Albany means well. Exhausted by privation and exertion
(the fact that he kills two assassins to the original Lear's one helps
prolong the suspense before rescue), he faces Albany with defiance which yet includes a plea for Cordelia. Albany is unable to
make him understand that there is no further cause for alarm,
and the King, pathetic and truculent, resolves to "hope no more."
This leads Albany to tell the story of Edgar's duel with Edmund,
and Lear interrupts with a regally imperious "And whither tends
this story?" He lapses again into a silence which persists for a
space of twenty-one lines, and is the last person of all to be con-
vinced. By these means, through Lear's changes from defiance to
pitifulness, to defiance again and then to joy, the final reconcilia-
tion is artfully withheld and the pathos of the scene gradually
stretched out, yet concentrated upon the protagonist.

Another sentimental effect is contrived by the way in which
Tate's speakers invariably turn the pathos back upon themselves.
It is characteristic that Edgar's anguished comment on the spectacle of his blinded father (IV.ii.5–10) should end, "When will the
measure of my woes be full?" Sometimes this effect is brought
about by making literal the original image. For example, Kent's

[46]Ibid., p. 68.

reply to Lear's threat in Shakespeare's I.i—"Kill thy physician and thy fee bestow upon the foul disease"—is changed by Tate to:

> . . . kill thy physician, Lear.
> Strike through my throat, yet with my latest breath
> I'll thunder in thine ear my just complaint,
> And tell thee to thy face that thou dost ill.
> (I.i.158–61)

The emphasis here is no longer squarely on Lear's folly but also on Kent's anticipated martyrdom. (In the emotional state evoked by the idea of Kent's being martyred, the difficulty of his thundering simultaneously to Lear's face and in his ear with his expiring gasp seems to have been overlooked.)

The most unashamedly sentimental effect in the adaptation is Cordelia's reappearance in III.ii. (Though it would scarcely seem necessary to increase the distress of Shakespeare's fourth act, which includes the Dover Cliff scene and the encounter between mad Lear and blind Gloucester, Tate elects in IV.ii to bring together Cordelia, Kent, Edgar and Gloster in a tearful encounter of outcasts.) Cordelia has been out of the play since I.i and it apparently seemed necessary to present her emphatically as the antithesis of her sisters. The picture she draws of herself with a dead Lear (dead, as usual, by anticipation) is in its details a verbal rendering of a *Pietà*:

> And I have only one poor boon to beg
> That you'd convey me to his breathless trunk:
> With my torn robes to wrap his hoary head,
> With my torn hair to bind his hands and feet,
> Then, with a shower of tears
> To wash his clay-smeared cheeks, and die beside him.
> (III.ii.85–90)

She has given herself over to the self-created mood; again we can see Tate striving for the effect of the final deaths in Shakespeare. But such an attempt, when the protagonists remain alive, tends at most to evoke distress without significance.

At times the devices get out of hand. To have Gloster, who will be blinded for treason, refer to Edgar throughout the early acts as "traitor" is simply irony; but after contriving the effect Tate feels compelled to increase it by giving Gloster a speech worked up from a general reference to the "drawing" or disembowelling of persons convicted of treason. The result is one of the most grotesque passages in the play:

> Fly, Edmund, seek him out, wind me into him
> That I may bite the traitor's heart, and fold
> His bleeding entrails on my vengeful arm.
>
> (I.i.282–84)

Yet the notes do not always jar. In a neat pathetic turn Gloster orders away his disguised son Edgar (III.iii.150). And Tate can at times exercise restraint. For example, the Captain's callous repetition, in Cordelia's own words, of her request to be hanged first, is dramatically effective:

CORDELIA.

> . . . I beg you to dispatch me first.

CAPTAIN.

> Comply with her request, dispatch her first.

And Lear's words to Gloster in the final scene, for example, are quiet and touching: "My poor dark Gloster."

James Hawkesworth, reviewing the elder Colman's sentimental play, *The English Merchant* (1767), wrote of the "higher pleasure" of tears:

> There is a luxury in tears that laughter can never taste; . . . they are an effusion of tenderness, complacency, admiration and joy excited by generous passion, untutored benevolence, and unexpected felicity.[47]

That is precisely the sentimental recipe which Tate has anticipated in the *History*. Generous passion there is in plenty, and unexpected felicity. Untutored benevolence is represented primarily by Kent: even though he commands Lear's troops and "exposes [his] life and fortunes" (V.iv.54) for his king like a Civil War Cavalier, it is the "rough, blunt fellow," the Cajus personality, who predominates. Edgar in disguise also shares in the quality; in Cordelia's sight he is something of a noble savage, as witness her reference to his "hallowed rags . . . and naked virtue" in III.iv.96. Where Shakespeare has reduced his aristocrats to complete desolation—to "the thing itself"—Tate's blue-blooded protagonists become in adversity something nearer the middle- or lower-class characters of sentimental drama.

[47]*The Gentleman's Magazine* (1767), p. 130.

It is significant that the play was later chosen for re-adaptation by George Colman the elder, a champion of sentimentalism. Colman, who set out to reconcile "the catastrophe of Tate to the story of Shakespeare," excised the love story but retained the happy ending and many of Tate's pathetic strokes such as those at IV.v.34–35 and 49–52, and V.iv.45–82. He knew that the contemporary public liked these effects. That his version failed and was long survived by Tate's suggests that the public preferred the love story as well. Nearly a century after Tate's adaptation, it was still "the general suffrage" which Samuel Johnson was inclined to obey in the matter of Tate's *Lear*:

> In the present case the publick has decided. Cordelia, from the time of Tate, has always retired with victory and felicity. And if my sensations could add any thing to the general suffrage, I might relate, that I was many years ago so shocked by Cordelia's death, that I know not whether I ever endured to read again the last scenes of the play till I undertook to revise them as an editor.[48]

Johnson recognized that Tate's *History of King Lear*, though not a play for all time, was nevertheless of its age.

The date of the first performance of *The History of King Lear* at the Duke's Theater, Dorset Garden, is a matter of dispute.[49] My own belief, based mainly upon a topical reference in the Prologue, is that the play was first produced around New Year 1680/81.[50] Few records and no reviews of performances of the play exist prior to 1700. It was given before King James at Whitehall on 9 May 1687 and 29 February 1688,[51] and seen at Drury Lane on 3 February 1699. The appearance of editions in 1689, 1699, and 1702 may indicate stage revivals. Betterton's biographer Charles Gildon says that *King Lear* was one of the

---

[48]*Johnson on Shakespeare*, pp. 161–62.

[49]In *Shakespearean Adaptations* (1922) Montague Summers says Tate's play first appeared "in the early spring of 1681"; in *Bibliography of the Restoration Drama* (1934) and *The Restoration Theatre* (1934), he opts for September 1680. Allardyce Nicoll (*Restoration Drama*, p. 434) conjectures "c. March 1681."

[50]See my article "An Augustan Stage-History: Nahum Tate's *King Lear*," pp. 36–37.

[51]Nicoll, *Restoration Drama*, p. 351.

plays in which Betterton "made some considerable figure." [52] But Thomas Davies has observed that

> No writer has taken notice of [Betterton's] exhibition of Lear; a part of equal consequence, and requiring as perfect skill in the player as any of them. I am almost tempted to believe that this tragedy, notwithstanding that Tate's alterations were approved, was not in such a good degree of favour with the public as *Hamlet, Othello,* and many other of our poet's dramas.[53]

Only two performances of Shakespeare's *King Lear* are known in Betterton's time.

But the record shows that Tate's version flourished after 1700. Between 1702 and the year of Tate's death, 1715, the adaptation was performed at least once each year except 1707. Tate's *Injured Love* (1707) could be advertised on the title page as being "by the author of *King Lear*." As the Restoration monopolistic system of playing rights to "Shakespeare's" plays (which included the adaptations) died out, rival productions of *The History of King Lear* were mounted at Drury Lane and Lincoln's Inn Fields. In the season 1720–21 seven performances of the adaptation averaged takings of over £75, very good returns in a season when twenty-two out of the sixty-six performances of Shakespeare lost money.

Every leading actor from Betterton through Macready played in Tate's version: Barton Booth, Anthony Boheme, Quin, Delane, Garrick, Spranger Barry, Kemble, and Edmund Kean. William Smith, Verbruggen, Wells, and Ryan played Edgar at various times; John Mills played Edmund, and Colley Cibber appeared as Gloster intermittently between 1709 and 1719. Garrick performed fifty-nine times as Lear in the Tate version, beginning in 1742, and chose the play for his own benefits on 18 February 1754, and 4 March 1755. On 28 October 1756 his own re-adapted version was first staged. Garrick retained the Tate plot but restored many of Shakespeare's lines, especially in the first three acts. The Fool was still omitted. The general effect of Garrick's cuts and revisions was to remove some of the logical thread of Tate's plot without completely restoring Shakespeare. The Garrick version was popular while Garrick himself played the leading role, but

---

[52]*The Life of Mr. Thomas Betterton* (London, 1710), pp. 174–75.
[53]*Dramatic Miscellanies*, 1:286.

further adaptation was not out of the question. In 1767 George Colman the elder set to work, and staged his version at Covent Garden in February 1768. Besides dispensing with Tate's love story, Colman sent Gloster off-stage to be blinded and deleted the Dover Cliff incident. He considered restoring the Fool, but feared that the inclusion of this character would cause the play to "sink into burlesque in the representation." His version had fifteen performances between 1768 and May 1773. Thus there could be seen, around 1770, three competing versions of *King Lear*, not one of which, strictly speaking, was Shakespeare's. In the autumn of 1770 Tate's version was at the Haymarket, 11 September; Colman's was at Covent Garden, 29 October; and Garrick's at Drury Lane on 31 October.

Spranger Barry replaced Colman's *Lear* with Tate's at Covent Garden in 1774, and after Garrick's death the Tate version was the one most frequently acted. Kemble played the lead in a revival of Garrick's adaptation in 1788; but when he became manager at Drury Lane he reverted to what was in nearly all points the Tate play, and acted in it at various times from 1792 onward. The printed version of Kemble's acting edition (1810) was advertised as "Shakespeare's *King Lear* as altered by N. Tate. Newly revised by J. P. Kemble." It shows some restoration of Shakespearean lines and omits the speech with which Tate's Edgar concludes the play; but the version is almost entirely Tate's. While Kemble was being acclaimed for his performances in this play (Mrs. Siddons was his Cordelia), Tate's adaptation, unaltered, was being offered at Covent Garden. The version presented by Kean at Drury Lane in 1822 was also substantially Tate's play.

But Kean eventually restored the tragic ending, on February 10, 1823. By John Genest's account the restoration of Shakespeare's catastrophe did not at first run smoothly, or have the desired effect, for

> Kean could not carry Mrs. W. West without difficulty—this is said to have set the audience into a laugh, which continued till the curtain dropt.[54]

In that performance, at least, Tate's doubts, expressed in the dedication, about the tragic ending were accidentally justified.

Kean's restoration was unsuccessful, and until Macready took

[54]*Some Account of the English Stage* (Bath, 1832), 9:186.

the leading role in 1834 and reintroduced almost all of Shakespeare's text, Tate's version was still given. Nor did Macready at first restore the Fool, believing the part to be unactable by a boy. But when it was suggested to him that a woman play the role, he assigned it to Priscilla Horton, a young actress with a fine singing voice, and Shakespeare's *King Lear* was presented complete on 25 January 1838.

Tate's adaptation was not, however, consigned to oblivion. The American actor Edwin Forrest offered it in London in March 1845. And traces of Tate's ordering of the scenes still survived. In Charles Kean's revival of *King Lear* in April 1858, Act One ended where Tate ends it, just after the famous cursing of Goneril, and Act Five opened with the tableau introduced by Tate to begin his IV.v: "A tent in the French camp. Lear on a bed asleep. Cordelia, Physician and others attending." In July 1949, Tate's *History of King Lear* was again presented in London, by the Oxford University players at the Fortune Theater, Drury Lane. This production was essentially a re-creation of Garrick's 1742 appearance in Tate's adaptation. The Garrick method—in the Tate version —was again re-created by the Stewart Headlam Players in Richmond, Yorkshire, and London in April and May 1966.

JAMES BLACK

University of Calgary

THE HISTORY OF KING LEAR

To My Esteemed Friend
Thomas Boteler, Esq.

Sir,

You have a natural right to this piece, since by your
advice I attempted the revival of it with alterations. Noth-   5
ing but the power of your persuasion, and my zeal for
all the remains of Shakespeare, could have wrought me
to so bold an undertaking. I found that the new-
modeling of this story would force me sometimes on the
difficult task of making the chiefest persons speak some-   10
thing like their character, on matter whereof I had no
ground in my author. Lear's real and Edgar's pretended
madness have so much of extravagant Nature (I know
not how else to express it) as could never have started
but from our Shakespeare's creating fancy. The images   15
and language are so odd and surprising, and yet so
agreeable and proper, that whilst we grant that none but
Shakespeare could have formed such conceptions, yet
we are satisfied that they were the only things in the
world that ought to be said on those occasions. I found   20
the whole to answer your account of it, a heap of jewels,
unstrung and unpolished, yet so dazzling in their disorder that I soon perceived I had seized a treasure. 'Twas
my good fortune to light on one expedient to rectify
what was wanting in the regularity and probability of the   25
tale, which was to run through the whole a love betwixt

26. whole a] *Q1;* whole, a *Q2;*
whole, as *Q3–5.*

---

2. *Thomas Boteler, Esq.*] Arthur H. Scouten identifies Thomas Boteler as
a cousin of Aston Cokain, whose *Trappolin Suppos'd a Prince* was adapted
by Tate into *A Duke and No Duke* in 1684 ("Aston Cokain and his Adapter
Nahum Tate" [Ph.D. diss., Louisiana State University, 1942], p. cxii). The
familiarity of Tate's address suggests that Montague Summers was incor-
rect in hazarding that Boteler was a nobleman "of the family of the Duke
of Ormond," (*Shakespearean Adaptations* [1922], p. 280). Among the con-
tributors to Dryden's edition of *Ovid's Epistles, Translated by Several Hands*
(1680), to which Tate contributed three pieces, is a "Mr. Butler;" so possibly the Boteler of this dedication was a member of a circle of minor poets
and translators, another of whom, Thomas Flatman, was a close friend of
Tate's.
14. *started*] sprung spontaneously to life.

1

Edgar and Cordelia, that never changed word with each other in the original. This renders Cordelia's indifference and her father's passion in the first scene probable. It likewise gives countenance to Edgar's disguise, making 30 that a generous design that was before a poor shift to save his life. The distress of the story is evidently heightened by it; and it particularly gave occasion of a new scene or two, of more success (perhaps) than merit. This method necessarily threw me on making the tale con- 35 clude in a success to the innocent distressed persons: otherwise I must have incumbered the stage with dead bodies, which conduct makes many tragedies conclude with unseasonable jests. Yet was I racked with no small fears for so bold a change, till I found it well received by 40 my audience; and if this will not satisfy the reader, I can produce an authority that questionless will. "Neither is it of so trivial an undertaking to make a tragedy end happily, for 'tis more difficult to save than 'tis to kill. The dagger and cup of poison are always in readiness; but to 45 bring the action to the last extremity, and then by probable means to recover all, will require the art and judgment of a writer, and cost him many a pang in the performance."

I have one thing more to apologize for, which is that I 50 have used less quaintness of expression even in the newest parts of this play. I confess 'twas design in me, partly to comply with my author's style to make the scenes of a piece, and partly to give it some resemblance of the time and persons here represented. This, sir, I 55 submit wholly to you, who are both a judge and master of style. Nature had exempted you before you went abroad from the morose saturnine humor of our country,

42-49. Neither . . . performance]   *Q1-5: Mr.* Dryd. *Pref. to the* Span.
identified marginally after ll. 42–44 in   Fryar.

---

30. *countenance*] credit, repute.
42–49. *Neither . . . performance*] This is identified in the margin as being from Dryden's *The Spanish Friar,* a tragicomedy first produced ca. November 1680 (*The London Stage,* Part I, p. 292) and listed in the *Term Catalogues* in Trinity term (June) 1681.
51. *quaintness of expression*] elegance in style or language.
58. *our country*] apparently Ireland.

and you brought home the refinedness of travel without
the affectation. Many faults I see in the following pages,   60
and question not but you will discover more; yet I will
presume so far on your friendship as to make the whole
a present to you, and subscribe myself

Your obliged friend
and humble servant,   65
N. TATE

THE PERSONS

KING LEAR	*Mr. Betterton*
GLOSTER	*Mr. Gillo*
KENT	*Mr. Wiltshire*
EDGAR	*Mr. Smith*
BASTARD	*Mr. Jo. Williams*
CORNWALL	*Mr. Norris*
ALBANY	*Mr. Bowman*
[BURGUNDY]	
GENTLEMAN-USHER	*Mr. Jevon*
[AN OLD MAN]	
[PHYSICIAN]	
GONERILL	*Mrs. Shadwell*
REGAN	*Lady Slingsby*
CORDELIA	*Mrs. Barry*
[ARANTE]	

GUARDS, OFFICERS, MESSENGERS [,TWO RUFFIANS], ATTENDANTS

*The parts enclosed in brackets are not
listed in Q1–5.*

Arante] In Tate's *Brutus of Alba* (1678) the Queen's confidante is named
Arante.

4

PROLOGUE

Since by mistakes your best delights are made
(For ev'n your wives can please in masquerade),
'Twere worth our while t'have drawn you in this day
By a new name to our old honest play;
But he that did this evening's treat prepare   5
Bluntly resolved beforehand to declare
Your entertainment should be most old fare,
Yet hopes, since in rich Shakespeare's soil it grew,
'Twill relish yet with those whose tastes are true,
And his ambition is to please a few.   10
If then this heap of flow'rs shall chance to wear
Fresh beauty in the order they now bear,
Ev'n this Shakespeare's praise; each rustic knows
'Mongst plenteous flow'rs a garland to compose,
Which strung by his coarse hand may fairer show,   15
But 'twas a pow'r divine first made 'em grow.
Why should these scenes lie hid, in which we find
What may at once divert and teach the mind?
Morals were always proper for the stage,
But are ev'n necessary in this age.   20
Poets must take the churches' teaching trade,
Since priests their province of intrigue invade;
But we the worst in this exchange have got,
In vain our poets preach, whilst churchmen plot.

15. his] *Q1;* this *Q2–5.*

The Prologue and Epilogue are reprinted in Tate's *Poems on Several Occasions* (1684).

2. *in masquerade*] in disguise.

13. *this*] i.e., "this is."

13. *knows*] knows how.

21–24. *Poets . . . plot*] The "Popish Plot" was disclosed in October 1678, and many priests—real or alleged—were implicated in the witchhunt that followed. Around the time of the first production of Tate's *King Lear* the Exclusion controversy was still a lively issue; and Oliver Plunket, Roman Catholic Primate of Ireland, had been brought to England (November, 1680) for arraignment and subsequent execution on a charge of conspiring to land a French army in Ireland.

KING LEAR
A TRAGEDY

ACT I

[I.i]   *[Lear's palace.]*
                          Enter Bastard *solus.*

BASTARD.
    Thou Nature, art my goddess; to thy law
    My services are bound. Why am I then
    Deprived of a son's right because I came not
    In the dull road that custom has prescribed?
    Why bastard, wherefore base, when I can boast   5
    A mind as gen'rous and a shape as true
    As honest madam's issue? Why are we
    Held base, who in the lusty stealth of nature
    Take fiercer qualities than what compound
    The scanted births of the stale marriage-bed?   10
    Well then, legitimate Edgar, to thy right
    Of law I will oppose a bastard's cunning.
    Our father's love is to the bastard Edmund
    As to legitimate Edgar. With success
    I've practiced yet on both their easy natures.
    Here comes the old man chafed with th'information
    Which last I forged against my brother Edgar:
    A tale so plausible, so boldly uttered,
    And heightened by such lucky accidents

King Lear A Tragedy] Despite the play's new name, *The History of King
Lear,* this head-title appears in all quartos.
  0.1. *Lear's palace*] Cf. l. 72.
  10. *scanted births*] meager products.
  15. *easy*] credulous.   19. *heightened*] made more credible.

Edmund ... dukes' step-son
's mother ?—— before marriage

That now the slightest circumstance confirms him,   20
And base-born Edmund spite of law inherits. [*Stands aside.*]

Enter Kent *and* Gloster.

GLOSTER.
    Nay, good my lord, your charity
    O'ershoots itself to plead in his behalf;
    You are yourself a father, and may feel
    The sting of disobedience from a son   25
    First-born and best beloved. Oh, villain Edgar!
KENT.
    Be not too rash, all may be forgery,
    And time yet clear the duty of your son.
GLOSTER.
    Plead with the seas, and reason down the winds,
    Yet shalt thou ne'er convince me; I have seen   30
    His foul designs through all a father's fondness.
    But be this light and thou my witnesses
    That I discard him here from my possessions,
    Divorce him from my heart, my blood and name.
BASTARD [*aside*].
    It works as I could wish; I'll show myself.   35
GLOSTER.
    Ha Edmund! Welcome, boy. O Kent, see here
    Inverted nature, Gloster's shame and glory.
    This by-born, the wild sally of my youth,
    Pursues me with all filial offices,
    Whilst Edgar, begged of Heaven and born in honor,   40
    Draws plagues on my white head that urge me still
    To curse in age the pleasure of my youth.
    Nay weep not, Edmund, for thy brother's crimes;
    O gen'rous boy, thou shar'st but half his blood,
    Yet lov'st beyond the kindness of a brother.   45
    But I'll reward thy virtue. Follow me.
    My lord, you wait the king, who comes resolved

21. S.D.] *this edn.; not in Q1–5.*   33. here] *Q1–2;* hear *Q3–5.*

28. *clear . . . duty*] i.e., make the dutifulness manifest.
38. *by-born*] variant of "by-blow," an illegitimate child.
38. *sally*] escapade.

To quit the toils of empire, and divide
His realms amongst his daughters. Heaven succeed it,
But much I fear the change.
KENT.   I grieve to see him   50
With such wild starts of passion hourly seized,
As renders majesty beneath itself.
GLOSTER.
Alas! 'tis the infirmity of his age.
Yet has his temper ever been unfixed,
Choleric and sudden— Hark, they approach.   55
                              Exeunt Gloster *and* Bastard.

Flourish. Enter Lear, Cornwall, Albany, Burgundy, Edgar,
Gonerill, Regan, Cordelia: Edgar *speaking to* Cordelia *at entrance.*

EDGAR.
Cordelia, royal fair, turn yet once more,
And ere successful Burgundy receive
The treasure of thy beauties from the king,
Ere happy Burgundy forever fold thee,
Cast back one pitying look on wretched Edgar.   60
CORDELIA.
Alas, what would the wretched Edgar with
The more unfortunate Cordelia
Who in obedience to a father's will
Flies from her Edgar's arms to Burgundy's?
LEAR.
Attend my lords of Albany and Cornwall   65
With princely Burgundy.
ALBANY.   We do, my liege.
LEAR.
Give me the map. Know, lords, we have divided
In three our kingdom, having now resolved
To disengage from our long toil of state,
Conferring all upon your younger years.   70
You, Burgundy, Cornwall, and Albany,
Long in our court have made your amorous sojourn

49. Heaven] *Q1–4;* Heavens *Q5.*   58. treasure] *Q1–4;* treasures *Q5.*
52. renders] *Q1, 5;* render *Q2–4.*   67. the] *Q1–2;* this *Q3–5.*

49. *succeed*] prosper.

9

And now are to be answered. —Tell me, my daughters,
Which of you loves us most, that we may place
Our largest bounty with the largest merit.   75
Gonerill, our eldest-born, speak first.

GONERILL.
Sir, I do love you more than words can utter,
Beyond what can be valued, rich or rare;
Nor liberty, nor sight, health, fame, or beauty
Are half so dear, my life for you were vile;   80
As much as child can love the best of fathers.

LEAR.
Of all these bounds, ev'n from this line to this,
With shady forests and wide-skirted meads,
We make thee lady; to thine and Albany's issue
Be this perpetual. —What says our second daughter?   85

REGAN.
My sister, sir, in part expressed my love,
For such as hers is mine, though more extended:
Sense has no other joy that I can relish,
I have my all in my dear liege's love!

LEAR.
Therefore to thee and thine hereditary   90
Remain this ample third of our fair kingdom.

CORDELIA *(aside)*.
Now comes my trial. How am I distressed,
That must with cold speech tempt the choleric king
Rather to leave me dowerless, than condemn me
To loathed embraces!   95

LEAR.
Speak now our last, not least in our dear love—
So ends my task of state—Cordelia, speak:
What canst thou say to win a richer third
That what thy sisters gained?

CORDELIA [*aside*].
Now must my love in words fall short of theirs   100

---

75. the] *Q1–3;* our *Q4–5.*

---

80. *my life . . . vile*] i.e., my life would be worthless without you. Possibly
Gonerill is given a garbled speech to suggest the extent of her mendacity
and Lear's infatuation.

10

As much as it exceeds in truth.   [*To* Lear.]   Nothing, my
   lord.

LEAR.
   Nothing can come of nothing; speak again.
CORDELIA.
   Unhappy am I that I can't dissemble.
   Sir, as I ought, I love Your Majesty;
   No more nor less.

LEAR.   Take heed, Cordelia,   105
   Thy fortunes are at stake; think better on't
   And mend thy speech a little.

CORDELIA.   O my liege,
   You gave me being, bred me, dearly love me;
   And I return my duty as I ought,
   Obey you, love you, and most honor you!   110
   Why have my sisters husbands, if they love you all?
   Happ'ly when I shall wed, the lord whose hand
   Shall take my plight will carry half my love.
   For I shall never marry, like my sisters,
   To love my father all.   115

LEAR.
   And goes thy heart with this?
   'Tis said that I am choleric. Judge me, gods,
   Is there not cause? Now, minion, I perceive
   The truth of what has been suggested to us:
   Thy fondness for the rebel son of Gloster,   120
   False to his father, as thou art to my hopes.
   And oh take heed, rash girl, lest we comply
   With thy fond wishes, which thou wilt too late
   Repent, for know our nature cannot brook
   A child so young and so ungentle.   125

CORDELIA.
   So young, my lord, and true.

LEAR.
   Thy truth then be thy dower,

104. I ought] *Q1–4;* ought I *Q5.*   *Q2–3.*
114. never] *Q1, 4–5;* never never   118. there] *Q1–3;* their *Q4–5.*

___

113. *plight*] troth-plight.
118. *minion*] a favorite child, but here used contemptuously.
123. *fond*] foolish.

11

For by the sacred sun and solemn night
I here disclaim all my paternal care,
And from this minute hold thee as a stranger   130
Both to my blood and favor.
KENT.   This is frenzy.
  Consider, good my liege—
LEAR.   Peace, Kent.
  Come not between a dragon and his rage.
  I loved her most, and in her tender trust
  Designed to have bestowed my age at ease!   135
  So be my grave my peace as here I give
  My heart from her, and with it all my wealth.
  My lords of Cornwall and of Albany,
  I do invest you jointly with full right
  In this fair third, Cordelia's forfeit dower.   140
  Mark me, my lords, observe our last resolve:
  Ourself, attended with an hundred knights,
  Will make abode with you in monthly course;
  The name alone of King remain with me,
  Yours be the execution and revenues.   145
  This is our final will, and to confirm it
  This coronet part between you.
KENT.   Royal Lear,
  Whom I have ever honored as my king,
  Loved as my father, as my master followed,
  And as my patron thought on in my prayers—   150
LEAR.
  Away, the bow is bent, make from the shaft.
KENT.
  No, let it fall and drench within my heart,
  Be Kent unmannerly when Lear is mad:
  Thy youngest daughter—
LEAR.   On thy life, no more!
KENT.
  What wilt thou do, old man?
LEAR.   Out of my sight!   155

139. with] *Q1–2;* in *Q3–5.*
154. thy] *Q1–2;* my *Q3–5.*

_____

152. *drench*] i.e., plunge.

12

KENT.
    See better first.
LEAR.   Now by the gods—
KENT.
    Now by the gods, rash king, thou swear'st in vain.
LEAR.
    Ha, traitor—
KENT.   Do, kill thy physician, Lear.
    Strike through my throat, yet with my latest breath
    I'll thunder in thine ear my just complaint,   160
    And tell thee to thy face that thou dost ill.
LEAR.
    Hear me, rash man, on thy allegiance hear me:
    Since thou hast striv'n to make us break our vow
    And pressed between our sentence and our power,
    Which nor our nature nor our place can bear,   165
    We banish thee forever from our sight
    And kingdom; if when three days are expired
    Thy hated trunk be found in our dominions,
    That moment is thy death. Away!
KENT.
    Why fare thee well, king. Since thou art resolved,   170
    I take thee at thy word, and will not stay
    To see thy fall; the gods protect the maid
    That truly thinks, and has most justly said.
    Thus to new climates my old truth I bear;
    Friendship lives hence, and banishment is here.   175
                                        Exit [Kent].
LEAR.
    Now Burgundy, you see her price is fall'n,
    Yet if the fondness of your passion still
    Affects her as she stands, dowerless, and lost
    In our esteem, she's yours; take her or leave her.
BURGUNDY.
    Pardon me, royal Lear, I but demand   180
    The dower yourself proposed, and here I take
    Cordelia by the hand, Duchess of Burgundy.

---

176. *price*] value.
178. *Affects*] loves.
178–79. *lost . . . esteem*] ruined in my estimation.

LEAR.

Then leave her, sir, for by a father's rage
I tell you all her wealth. Away!

BURGUNDY.

Then sir be pleased to charge the breach   185
Of our alliance on your own will,
Not my inconstancy.

Exeunt. Manent Edgar *and* Cordelia.

EDGAR.

Has Heaven then weighed the merit of my love,
Or is't the raving of my sickly thought?
Could Burgundy forgo so rich a prize   190
And leave her to despairing Edgar's arms?
Have I thy hand, Cordelia, do I clasp it,
The hand that was this minute to have joined
My hated rival's? Do I kneel before thee
And offer at thy feet my panting heart?   195
Smile, princess, and convince me, for as yet
I doubt, and dare not trust the dazzling joy.

CORDELIA.

Some comfort yet that 'twas no vicious blot
That has deprived me of a father's grace,
But merely want of that that makes me rich   200
In wanting it, a smooth professing tongue:
O sisters, I am loath to call your fault
As it deserves; but use our father well,
And wronged Cordelia never shall repine.

EDGAR.

O heavenly maid that art thyself thy dower,   205
Richer in virtue than the stars in light,
If Edgar's humble fortunes may be graced
With thy acceptance, at thy feet he lays 'em.
Ha, my Cordelia! Dost thou turn away?
What have I done t'offend thee?   210

CORDELIA.

Talked of love.

---

200. that that] *Q1–3;* that which   202. sisters] *Q1–4;* Sister *Q5.*
Q4–5.

---

199. *grace*] favor and goodwill.   203. *call*] name.

EDGAR.

    Then I've offended oft, Cordelia too

    Has oft permitted me so to offend.

CORDELIA.

    When, Edgar, I permitted your addresses,

    I was the darling daughter of a king;   215

    Nor can I now forget my royal birth,

    And live dependent on my lover's fortune.

    I cannot to so low a fate submit;

    And therefore study to forget your passion,

    And trouble me upon this theme no more.   220

EDGAR.

    Thus majesty takes most state in distress!

    How are we tossed on Fortune's fickle flood!

    The wave that with surprising kindness brought

    The dear wreck to my arms, has snatched it back,

    And left me mourning on the barren shore.   225

CORDELIA *(aside)*.

    This baseness of th'ignoble Burgundy

    Draws just suspicion on the race of men.

    His love was int'rest, so may Edgar's be,

    And he but with more compliment dissemble.

    If so, I shall oblige him by denying.   230

    But if his love be fixed, such constant flame

    As warms our breasts: if such I find his passion,

    My heart as grateful to his truth shall be,

    And cold Cordelia prove as kind as he.   *Exit* [Cordelia].

Enter Bastard *hastily*.

BASTARD.

    Brother, I've found you in a lucky minute;   235

    Fly and be safe, some villain has incensed

    Our father against your life.

EDGAR.

    Distressed Cordelia! but oh! more cruel!

BASTARD.

    Hear me sir, your life, your life's in danger.

234. cold] *Q1–2;* could *Q3–5.*

---

  228. *int'rest*] selfish regard for his own profit.

  233. *grateful*] responsive.

EDGAR.

> A resolve so sudden   240
> And of such black importance!

BASTARD.   'Twas not sudden,

> Some villain has of long time laid the train.

EDGAR.

> And yet perhaps 'twas but pretended coldness,
> To try how far my passion would pursue.

BASTARD.

> He hears me not; wake, wake sir.

EDGAR.   Say ye, brother?—   245

> No tears, good Edmund; if thou bring'st me tidings
> To strike me dead, for charity delay not.
> That present will befit so kind a hand.

BASTARD.

> Your danger, sir, comes on so fast
> That I want time t'inform you; but retire   250
> Whilst I take care to turn the pressing stream.
> O gods! For Heaven's sake, sir.

EDGAR.

> Pardon me, sir, a serious thought
> Had seized me, but I think you talked of danger
> And wished me to retire. Must all our vows   255
> End thus!—Friend, I obey you—O Cordelia!

BASTARD.

> Ha! ha! Fond man, such credulous honesty
> Lessens the glory of my artifice;
> His nature is so far from doing wrongs
> That he suspects none. If this letter speed   260
> And pass for Edgar's, as himself would own
> The counterfeit but for the foul contents,
> Then my designs are perfect. — Here comes Gloster.

> > *Enter* Gloster.

GLOSTER.

> Stay Edmund, turn, what paper were you reading?

BASTARD.

> A trifle, sir.   265

GLOSTER.

> What needed then that terrible dispatch of it into your
> pocket? Come, produce it sir.

16

BASTARD.

    A letter from my brother, sir, I had
    Just broke the seal but knew not the contents.
    Yet, fearing they might prove to blame,   270
    Endeavored to conceal it from your sight.

GLOSTER.

    'Tis Edgar's character.   *Reads.*
    "This policy of fathers is intolerable, that keeps our for-
    tunes from us till age will not suffer us to enjoy 'em. I am
    weary of the tyranny: come to me that of this I may 275
    speak more. If our father would sleep till I waked him,
    you should enjoy half his possessions, and live beloved of
    your brother
                               E DGAR."
    "Slept till I waked him, you should enjoy
    Half his possessions"—Edgar to write this   280
    'Gainst his indulgent father! Death and hell!
    Fly, Edmund, seek him out, wind me into him
    That I may bite the traitor's heart, and fold
    His bleeding entrails on my vengeful arm.

BASTARD.

    Perhaps 'twas writ, my lord, to prove my virtue.   285

GLOSTER.

    These late eclipses of the sun and moon
    Can bode no less; love cools, and friendship fails,
    In cities mutiny, in countries discord,
    The bond of nature cracked 'twixt son and father.
    Find out the villain, do it carefully   290
    And it shall lose thee nothing.   *Exit* [Gloster].

BASTARD.

    So, now my project's firm, but to make sure
    I'll throw in one proof more and that a bold one:
    I'll place old Gloster where he shall o'erhear us
    Confer of this design, whilst, to his thinking,   295
    Deluded Edgar shall accuse himself.
    Be honesty my int'rest and I can
    Be honest too; and what saint so divine
    That will successful villainy decline!   *Exit.*

279. waked] *Q2–5* (wak'd); wake *Q1.*

---

272. *character*] handwriting.   285. *prove*] test.

[I.ii]   *The Duke of Albany's palace.*
                          Enter Kent, *disguised.*

KENT.

    Now banished Kent, if thou canst pay thy duty
    In this disguise where thou dost stand condemned,
    Thy master Lear shall find thee full of labors.

Enter Lear *attended.*

LEAR.

    In there, and tell our daughter we are here.
    Now, what art thou?

KENT.   A man, sir.   5

LEAR.

    What dost thou profess, or wouldst with us?

KENT.

    I do profess to be no less than I seem, to serve him truly
    that puts me in trust, to love him that's honest, to con-
    verse with him that's wise and speaks little, to fight when
    I can't choose; and to eat no fish.   10

LEAR.

    I say, what art thou?

KENT.

    A very honest-hearted fellow, and as poor as the king.

LEAR.

    Then art thou poor indeed. What canst thou do?

KENT.

    I can keep honest counsel, mar a curious tale in the
    telling, deliver a plain message bluntly. That which ordi- 15
    nary men are fit for I am qualified in, and the best of me
    is diligence.

LEAR.

    Follow me, thou shalt serve me.

Enter one of Gonerill's Gentlemen.

                          Now sir?

GENTLEMAN.   Sir—

                        Exit. Kent *runs after him.*

I.ii.] *scene division not in Q1–5.*   4. here.] *Q2–5;* here *Q1.*

0.1. *palace*] See also l. 56.   10. *eat no fish*] be a Protestant.

LEAR.

What says the fellow? Call the clatpole back. [*Exit* Servant.].

ATTENDANT.

My lord I know not, but methinks Your Highness is   20
entertained with slender ceremony.

SERVANT [returning].

He says, my lord, your daughter is not well.

LEAR.

Why came not the slave back when I called him?

SERVANT.

My lord, he answered me i'th' surliest manner
That he would not.   25

Re-enter Gentleman, *brought in by* Kent.

LEAR.

I hope our daughter did not so instruct him.
Now, who am I sir?

GENTLEMAN.

My lady's father.

LEAR.   My lord's knave—   *Strikes him.*

Gonerill *at the entrance.*

GENTLEMAN.

I'll not be struck, my lord.

KENT.

Nor tripped neither, thou vile civet-box.   30
                              Strikes up his heels.

GONERILL [*coming forward*].

By day and night, this is insufferable;
I will not bear it.

LEAR.

Now, daughter, why that frontlet on?
Speak, does that frown become our presence?

---

19. Call the clatpole] *Q1–3;* Call me   *following* l. *34 in Q3–5.*
the Clodpole *Q4–5.*   33. frontlet] *Q1–2, 4–5;* frontless
29–30. I'll … civet-box] *Q1–2; set as*   *Q3.*

---

19. *clatpole*] blockhead.
30. *civet-box*] scent-box; like "essence bottle" (II.iii.29) and "muss-cat"
(II.iii.31), used opprobriously.

GONERILL.

    Sir, this licentious insolence of your servants   35
    Is most unseemly; hourly they break out
    In quarrels bred by their unbounded riots.
    I had fair hope by making this known to you
    T'have had a quick redress, but find too late
    That you protect and countenance their outrage.   40
    And therefore, sir, I take this freedom, which
    Necessity makes discreet.

LEAR.

    Are you our daughter?

GONERILL.

    Come, sir, let me entreat you to make use
    Of your discretion, and put off betimes   45
    This disposition that of late transforms you
    From what you rightly are.

LEAR.

    Does any here know me? Why, this is not Lear.
    Does Lear walk thus? Speak thus? Where are his eyes?
    Who is it that can tell me who I am?   50

GONERILL.

    Come, sir, this admiration's much o'th'savor
    Of other your new humors. I beseech you
    To understand my purposes aright.
    As you are old, you should be staid and wise.
    Here do you keep an hundred knights and squires,   55
    Men so debauched and bold that this our palace
    Shows like a riotous inn, a tavern, brothel.
    Be then advised by her that else will take
    The thing she begs, to lessen your attendance.
    Take half away, and see that the remainder   60
    Be such as may befit your age, and know
    Themselves and you.

LEAR.   Darkness and devils!

---

51. savor] *Q1–2, 4–5;* favour *Q3.*   That which *Q2–5.*
59. The thing] *this edn.;* The *Q1;*   60. away] *Q2–5;* a way *Q1.*

---

59. *The thing*] Evidently a word was omitted here by the Q1 compositor; the Q2 compositor seems to have repaired the omission with a new phrase (see textual note above). Since Shakespeare's *Lear* has "the thing," and Tate likely was following Shakespeare, I have supplied *thing* here.

Saddle my horses, call my train together.
Degenerate viper, I'll not stay with thee;
I yet have left a daughter— Serpent, monster,   65
Lessen my train, and call'em riotous?
All men approved of choice and rarest parts,
That each particular of duty know—
How small, Cordelia, was thy fault! O Lear,
Beat at this gate that let thy folly in,   70
And thy dear judgment out. Go, go, my people.
                        Going off meets Albany *entering.*
Ingrateful duke, was this your will?
ALBANY.   What, sir?
LEAR.
Death! fifty of my followers at a clap!
ALBANY.
The matter, madam?
GONERILL.
Never afflict yourself to know the cause,   75
But give his dotage way.
LEAR.   Blasts upon thee,
Th'untented woundings of a father's curse
Pierce every sense about thee. Old fond eyes,
Lament this cause again, I'll pluck ye out
And cast ye with the waters that ye lose   80
To temper clay— No, gorgon, thou shalt find
That I'll resume the shape which thou dost think
I have cast off forever.
GONERILL [*to* Albany].   Mark ye that.
LEAR.
Hear Nature!
Dear goddess, hear, and if thou dost intend   85
To make that creature fruitful, change thy purpose;
Pronounce upon her womb the barren curse,
That from her blasted body never spring
A babe to honor her. But if she must bring forth,
Defeat her joy with some distorted birth   90
Or monstrous form, the prodigy o'th'time,

---

88. *blasted*] blighted.
90. *Defeat*] disfigure.

21

And so perverse of spirit, that it may live
Her torment as 'twas born, to fret her cheeks
With constant tears, and wrinkle her young brow.
Turn all her mother's pains to shame and scorn   95
That she may curse her crime too late, and feel
How sharper than a serpent's tooth it is
To have a thankless child! Away, away.   *Exit cum suis.*

GONERILL.
Presuming thus upon his numerous train
He thinks to play the tyrant here, and hold   100
Our lives at will.

ALBANY.   Well, you may bear too far.   *Exeunt.*

End of the First Act

play] *Q1–3, 5;* ploy Q4.

92–93. *that . . . born*] i.e., that it may torment her through life as it did at
its birth.

93. *fret*] wear away.

98. S.D. *cum suis*] "with his," i.e., with his followers.

ACT II

Gloster's house.
Enter Bastard.

BASTARD.

    The duke comes here tonight, I'll take advantage
    Of his arrival to complete my project.
    Brother, a word. Come forth; 'tis I, your friend.

Enter Edgar.

    My father watches for you, fly this place.
    Intelligence is giv'n where you are hid.   5
    Take the advantage of the night; bethink ye,
    Have you not spoke against the Duke of Cornwall
    Something might show you a favorer of
    Duke Albany's party?

EDGAR.   Nothing, why ask you?

BASTARD.

    Because he's coming here tonight in haste   10
    And Regan with him— Hark! the guards, away.

EDGAR.

    Let 'em come on, I'll stay and clear myself.

BASTARD.

    Your innocence at leisure may be heard,
    But Gloster's storming rage as yet is deaf,
    And you may perish ere allowed the hearing.   15

Exit Edgar.

    Gloster comes yonder: now to my feigned scuffle—
    Yield, come before my father! Lights here, lights!—
    Some blood drawn on me would beget opinion

Stabs his arm.

    Of our more fierce encounter. I have seen
    Drunkards do more than this in sport.   20

Enter Gloster *and servants.*

GLOSTER.

    Now, Edmund, where's the traitor?

---

5. you are] *Q1–2;* your *Q3;* you're   7. you] *Q4–5; om. Q1–3. Q4–5.*

BASTARD.   That name, sir,
     Strikes horror through me; but my brother, sir,
     Stood here i'th'dark.
GLOSTER.
     Thou bleed'st. [*To servants.*] Pursue the villain
     And bring him piecemeal to me.
BASTARD.   Sir, he's fled.   25
GLOSTER.
     Let him fly far, this kingdom shall not hide him.
     The noble duke, my patron, comes tonight;
     By his authority I will proclaim
     Rewards for him that brings him to the stake,
     And death for the concealer.   30
     Then of my lands, loyal and natural boy,
     I'll work the means to make thee capable.   *Exeunt.*

[II.ii]   [*Before Gloster's house.*]
     Enter Kent (*disguised still*) *and Gonerill's* Gentleman, *severally.*

GENTLEMAN.
     Good morrow friend, belong'st thou to this house?
KENT.
     Ask them will answer thee.
GENTLEMAN.
     Where may we set our horses?
KENT.
     I'th'mire.
GENTLEMAN.
     I am in haste. Prithee, an thou lov'st me, tell me.   5
KENT.
     I love thee not.
GENTLEMAN.
     Why then, I care not for thee.
KENT.
     An I had thee in Lipsbury Pinfold, I'd make thee care
     for me.

---

29. stake] *Q1–2;* stage *Q3–5.*   II.ii.] *scene division not in Q1–5.*

32. *capable*] i.e., of inheriting.

8. *Lipsbury pinfold*] "Lipsbury," also in Shakespeare's II.ii.8, has never
been identified. A pinfold is a pen for stray cattle. Kent means "If I had you
in a private place . . . ."

24

GENTLEMAN.

What dost thou mean? I know thee not.   10

KENT.

But, minion, I know thee.

GENTLEMAN.

What dost thou know me for?

KENT.

For a base, proud, beggarly, white-livered, glass-gazing,
superserviceable, finical rogue; one that would be a
pimp in way of good service, and art nothing but a com- 15
position of knave, beggar, coward pander—

GENTLEMAN.

What a monstrous fellow art thou to rail at one that is
neither known of thee nor knows thee!

KENT.

Impudent slave, not know me, who but two days since
tripped up thy heels before the king! Draw, miscreant, 20
or I'll make the moon shine through thee.

GENTLEMAN.

What means the fellow? Why prithee, prithee; I tell thee
I have nothing to do with thee.

KENT.

I know your rogueship's office. You come with letters
against the king, taking my young Lady Vanity's part 25
against her royal father. Draw, rascal.

GENTLEMAN.

Murther! murther! help, ho!

KENT.

Dost thou scream, peacock? Strike, puppet, stand, dapper slave.

GENTLEMAN.

Help hea'! murther, help!   *Exit. Kent *after him.* 30

27–30. ho! . . . help!] *Q1–2; om.*
Q3–5.

---

13. *glass-gazing*] vain, foppish.

14. *superserviceable*] performing (ill) service beyond what is required.
Cf. IV.iv. 199–201.

14. *finical*] affectedly fastidious.

25. *Lady Vanity*] Gonerill. Lady Vanity is a well-known vice in morality
plays and interludes, such as *The Marriage of Wit and Wisdom*.

28–29. *dapper*] sprucely dressed, here used opprobriously.

[II.iii]   [*The same.*]

Flourish. Enter Duke of Cornwall, Regan, *attended.* [*To them*] Gloster, Bastard.

GLOSTER.
     All welcome to Your Graces, you do me honor.
DUKE.
     Gloster, w'ave heard with sorrow that your life
     Has been attempted by your impious son,
     But Edmund here has paid you strictest duty.
GLOSTER.
     He did betray his practice, and received   5
     The hurt you see, striving to apprehend him.
DUKE.
     Is he pursued?
GLOSTER.   He is, my lord.
REGAN.
     Use our authority to apprehend
     The traitor and do justice on his head.
     For you, Edmund, that have so signalized   10
     Your virtue, you from henceforth shall be ours;
     Natures of such firm trust we much shall need.—
     (*Aside.*) A charming youth, and worth my further thought.
DUKE.
     Lay comforts, noble Gloster, to your breast,
     As we to ours. This night be spent in revels.   15
     We choose you, Gloster, for our host tonight,
     A troublesome expression of our love.
     On, to the sports before us— Who are these?

               Enter the Gentleman *pursued by* Kent.
GLOSTER.
     Now, what's the matter?
DUKE.
     Keep peace upon your lives, he dies that strikes.   20
     Whence and what are ye?
ATTENDANT.
     Sir, they are messengers: the one from your sister, the
     other from the king.

II.iii.] *scene division not in Q1–5.*   4. you] *Q1–2, 4–5;* your *Q3.*

17. *troublesome*] i.e., an imposition upon Gloster.

DUKE.

    Your difference? Speak.

GENTLEMAN.   I'm scarce in breath, my lord.

KENT.

    No marvel, you have so bestirred your valor.   25
    Nature disclaims the dastard, a tailor made him.

DUKE.

    Speak yet, how grew your quarrel?

GENTLEMAN.

    Sir, this old ruffian here, whose life I spared
    In pity to his beard—

KENT.   Thou essence bottle!

    In pity to my beard?— Your leave, my lord,   30
    And I will tread the muss-cat into mortar.

DUKE.

    Know'st thou our presence?

KENT.

    Yes, sir, but anger has a privilege.

DUKE.

    Why art thou angry?

KENT.

    That such a slave as this should wear a sword   35
    And have no courage; office and no honesty.
    Not frost and fire hold more antipathy
    Than I and such a knave.

GLOSTER.

    Why dost thou call him knave?

KENT.

    His countenance likes me not.   40

DUKE.

    No more perhaps does mine, nor his or hers.

KENT.

    Plain-dealing is my trade, and to be plain, sir,
    I have seen better faces in my time

---

35. wear] *Q1–2, 5;* were *Q3–4.*

---

  26. *dastard*] a malicious coward.
  26. *a tailor made him*] i.e., he is nothing but external appearances.
  29. *essence bottle*] perfume bottle.
  31. *muss-cat*] musk-cat or civet-cat, the animal from which the base for perfume was extracted.

    Than stands on any shoulders now before me.

REGAN.

       This is some fellow that, having once been praised   45
       For bluntness, since affects a saucy rudeness;
       But I have known one of these surly knaves
       That in his plainness harbored more design
       Than twenty cringing complimenting minions.

DUKE.

       What's the offense you gave him?   50

GENTLEMAN.

       Never any, sir.
       It pleased the king his master lately
       To strike me on a slender misconstruction;
       Whilst watching his advantage this old lurcher
       Tripped me behind, for which the king extolled him;   55
       And, flushed with the honor of this bold exploit,
       Drew on me here again.

DUKE.

       Bring forth the stocks.   [*To* Kent.]   We'll teach you.

KENT.

       Sir, I'm too old to learn;
       Call not the stocks for me, I serve the king,   60
       On whose employment I was sent to you.
       You'll show too small respect, and too bold malice
       Against the person of my royal master,
       Stocking his messenger.

DUKE.

       Bring forth the stocks, as I have life and honor,   65
       There shall he sit till noon.

REGAN.

       Till noon, my lord? till night, and all night too.

KENT.

       Why madam, if I were your father's dog
       You would not use me so.

REGAN.   Sir, being his knave, I will.

GLOSTER.

       Let me beseech Your Graces to forbear him;   70
       His fault is much, and the good king his master

---

54. *lurcher*] rogue (Kersey).

Will check him for't, but needs must take it ill
To be thus slighted in his messenger.

DUKE.
We'll answer that;
Our sister may receive it worse to have   75
Her gentleman assaulted. To our business lead.
Exeunt [all but Gloster *and* Kent.]

GLOSTER.
I am sorry for thee, friend, 'tis the duke's pleasure,
Whose dispostion will not be controlled;
But I'll entreat for thee.

KENT.   Pray do not, sir.
I have watched and traveled hard,   80
Some time I shall sleep out, the rest I'll whistle:
Farewell t'ye, sir.   *Exit* Gloster.
All weary and o'er-watched,
I feel the drowsy guest steal on me. Take
Advantage, heavy eyes, of this kind slumber,
Not to behold this vile and shameful lodging.   *Sleeps.*   85

[II.iv]   [*A heath.*]
Enter Edgar.

EDGAR.
I heard myself proclaimed,
And by the friendly hollow of a tree
Escaped the hunt. No port is free, no place
Where guards and most unusual vigilance
Do not attend to take me. How easy now   5
'Twere to defeat the malice of my trail,
And leave my griefs on my sword's reeking point.
But love detains me from death's peaceful cell,
Still whispering me Cordelia's in distress.
Unkind as she is I cannot see her wretched,   10
But must be near to wait upon her fortune.
Who knows but the white minute yet may come
When Edgar may do service to Cordelia;

76.1. *Exeunt*] *this edn.; Exit Q1–5.*   3. Escaped] *Q1* (Escapt); Escape
II.iv.] *scene division not in Q1–5.*   *Q2–5.*

12. *white minute*] auspicious occasion, opportunity.

29

That charming hope still ties me to the oar
Of painful life, and makes me, too, submit   15
To th'humblest shifts to keep that life afoot.
My face I will besmear and knit my locks;
The country gives me proof and precedent
Of bedlam beggars, who with roaring voices
Strike in their numbed and mortified bare arms   20
Pins, iron spikes, thorns, sprigs of rosemary,
And thus from sheep-cotes, villages, and mills,
Sometimes with prayers, sometimes with lunatic bans
Enforce their charity. Poor Tyrligod! poor Tom!
That's something yet; Edgar I am no more.   *Exit.*   25

[II.v]   [*Before Gloster's house.*]
                    Kent *in the stocks still; enter* Lear *attended.*

LEAR.

'Tis strange that they should so depart from home
And not send back our messenger.

KENT.

Hail, noble master.

LEAR.

How? Mak'st thou this shame thy pastime?
What's he that has so much mistook thy place   5
To set thee here?

KENT.

It is both he and she, sir, your son and daughter.

LEAR.

No.

KENT.   Yes.

LEAR.   No I say.

KENT.   I say yea.

LEAR.

By Jupiter, I swear no.

KENT.

By Juno I swear, I swear ay.   10

15. too, submit] *Q1*; to submit   II.v.] *scene division not in Q1–5.*
Q2–5.   10. ay] *Q2–5;* I *Q1.*

24. *Tyrligod*] a name of unexplained origin; Edgar is practicing the
beggar's whine.

LEAR.

They durst not do't,
Thy could not, would not do't; 'tis worse than murder
To do upon respect such violent outrage.
Resolve me with all modest haste which way
Thou mayst deserve, or they impose this usage.   15

KENT.

My lord, when at their home
I did commend Your Highness' letters to them,
Ere I was ris'n, arrived another post
Steered in his haste, breathless and panting forth
From Gonerill his mistress salutations.   20
Whose message being delivered, they took horse,
Commanding me to follow and attend
The leisure of their answer, which I did.
But meeting here that other messenger
Whose welcome I perceived had poisoned mine,   25
Being the very fellow that of late
Had shown such rudeness to Your Highness, I,
Having more man than wit about me, drew,
On which he raised the house with coward cries.
This was the trespass which your son and daughter   30
Thought worth the shame you see it suffer here.

LEAR.

Oh! how this spleen swells upward to my heart
And heaves for passage— Down thou climbing rage!
They element's below. Where is this daughter?

KENT.

Within, sir, at a masque.

Enter Gloster.

LEAR.   Now Gloster?— [*They converse apart.*]
                                            Ha!   35
Deny to speak with me? Th'are sick, th'are weary,
They have traveled hard tonight—mere fetches!
Bring me a better answer.

14. modest] *Q1–2, 4–5;* moded *Q3.*   29. coward] *Q1–2;* cowards *Q3–5.*
24. here] *not in Q1–5.*

---

19. *Steered*] dialect form of "stirred" (*OED*), agitated.
32. *spleen*] passion.

GLOSTER.   My dear lord,
    You know the fiery quality of the duke—
LEAR.
    Vengeance! Death, plague, confusion!   40
    Fiery? what quality? Why Gloster, Gloster,
    I'd speak with the Duke of Cornwall and his wife.
GLOSTER.
    I have informed 'em so.
LEAR.
    Informed 'em! Dost thou understand me, man?
    I tell thee, Gloster—
GLOSTER.   Ay, my good lord.   45
LEAR.
    The king would speak with Cornwall, the dear father
    Would with his daughter speak, commands her service.
    Are they informed of this? My breath and blood!
    Fiery! the fiery duke! Tell the hot duke—
    No, but not yet, may be he is not well: 50
    Infirmity does still neglect all office.
    I beg his pardon, and I'll chide my rashness
    That took the indisposed and sickly fit
    For the sound man. But wherefore sits he there?
    Death on my state! this act convinces me   55
    That this retiredness of the duke and her
    Is plain contempt. Give me my servant forth,
    Go tell the duke and's wife I'd speak with 'em.
    Now, instantly, bid 'em come forth and hear me,
    Or at their chamber door I'll beat the drum   60
    Till it cry sleep to death—

                    Enter Cornwall *and* Regan.

                    Oh! are ye come?

DUKE.
    Health to the king.
REGAN.
    I am glad to see Your Highness.
LEAR.
    Regan, I think you are, I know what cause
    I have to think so; shouldst thou not be glad   65
    I would divorce me from thy mother's tomb.

Beloved Regan, thou wilt shake to hear
What I shall utter: thou couldst ne'er ha' thought it.
Thy sister's naught, O Regan, she has tied
                              Kent *here set at liberty.*
Ingratitude, like a keen vulture, here.   70
I scarce can speak to thee.

REGAN.

I pray you, sir, take patience; I have hope
That you know less to value her desert
Than she to slack her duty.

LEAR.   Ha! how's that?

REGAN.

I cannot think my sister in the least   75
Would fail in her respects, but if perchance
She has restrained the riots of your followers,
'Tis on such grounds, and to such wholesome ends.
As clears her from all blame.

LEAR.

My curses on her.

REGAN.   O sir, you are old   80
And should content you to be ruled and led
By some discretion that discerns your state
Better than you yourself. Therefore, sir,
Return to our sister, and say you have wronged her.

LEAR.

Ha! ask her forgiveness?   85
No, no, 'twas my mistake; thou didst not mean so.
Dear daughter, I confess that I am old;
Age is unnecessary, but thou art good,
And wilt dispense with my infirmity.

REGAN.

Good sir, no more of these unsightly passions.   90
Return back to our sister.

LEAR.   Never, Regan.
She has abated me of half my train,
Looked black upon me, stabbed me with her tongue;
All the stored vengeances of Heaven fall

79. clears] *Q1–2;* clear *Q3–5.*   92. of half] *Q3–5;* of half of *Q1–2.*

89. *dispense with*] pardon.

On her ingrateful head! Strike her young bones,   95
Ye taking airs, with lameness.

REGAN.

O the blest gods! Thus will you wish on me
When the rash mood—

LEAR.

No, Regan, thou shalt never have my curse;
Thy tender nature cannot give thee o'er   100
To such impiety. Thou better know'st
The offices of nature, bond of childhood,
And dues of gratitude. Thou bear'st in mind
The half o'th'kingdom which our love conferred
On thee and thine.

REGAN.   Good sir, to th'purpose.   105

LEAR.

Who put my man i'th'stocks?   [*Trumpet.*]

DUKE.   What trumpet's that?

REGAN.

I know't, my sister's, this confirms her letters.

                    Enter Gonerill's Gentleman.

Sir, is your lady come?

LEAR.   More torture still?
This is a slave whose easy-borrowed pride
Dwells in the fickle grace of her he follows;   110
A fashion-fop that spends the day in dressing,
And all to bear his lady's flattering message;
That can deliver with a grace her lie,
And with as bold a face bring back a greater.
Out, varlet, from my sight.

DUKE.   What means your grace?   115

LEAR.

Who stocked my servant? Regan, I have hope
Thou didst not know it.

                    Enter Gonerill.

                        Who comes here? Oh Heavens!
If you do love old men, if your sweet sway

---

106. put] *Q1–2; but Q3–5.*

Allow obedience, if yourselves are old,
Make it your cause, send down amd take my part.   120
Why, gorgon, dost thou come to haunt me here?
Art not ashamed to look upon this beard?
Darkness upon my eyes, they play me false;
O Regan, wilt thou take her by the hand?

GONERILL.

Why not by th'hand, sir? How have I offended?   125
All's not offense that indiscretion finds,
And dotage terms so.

LEAR.   Heart, thou art too tough.

REGAN.

I pray you, sir, being old, confess you are so.
If till the expiration of your month
You will return and sojourn with our sister,   130
Dismissing half your train, come then to me.
I am now from home, and out of that provision
That shall be needful for your entertainment.

LEAR.

Return with her and fifty knights dismissed?
No, rather I'll forswear all roofs, and choose   135
To be companion to the midnight wolf,
My naked head exposed to th'merciless air,
Than have my smallest wants supplied by her.

GONERILL

At your choice, sir.

LEAR.

Now I prithee, daughter, do not make me mad.   140
I will not trouble thee, my child, farewell,
We'll meet no more, no more see one another.
Let shame come when it will, I do not call it.
I do not bid the thunder-bearer strike,
Nor tell tales of thee to avenging Heaven.   145
Mend when thou canst, be better at thy leisure.
I can be patient, I can stay with Regan,
I, and my hundred knights.

REGAN.   Your pardon, sir.

---

130. our] *Q5;* your *Q1–4.*   133. shall] *Q1–2;* all *Q3–5.*

144. *Thunder-bearer*] i.e., Jupiter.

I looked not for you yet, nor am provided
For your fit welcome.   150
LEAR.
　　Is this well spoken now?
REGAN.
　　My sister treats you fair; what! fifty followers?
　　Is it not well? What should you need of more?
GONERILL.
　　Why might not you, my lord, receive attendance
　　From those whom she calls servants, or from mine?   155
REGAN.
　　Why not, my lord? If then they chance to slack you
　　We could control 'em. If you come to me—
　　For now I see the danger—I entreat you
　　To bring but five and twenty; to no more
　　Will I give place.   160
LEAR.
　　Hold now my temper, stand this bolt unmoved
　　And I am thunder-proof.
　　The wicked when compared with the more wicked
　　Seem beautiful, and not to be the worst
　　Stands in some rank of praise. Now, Gonerill,   165
　　Thou art innocent again, I'll go with thee.
　　Thy fifty yet does double five and twenty,
　　And thou art twice her love.
GONERILL.   Hear me, my lord,
　　What need you five and twenty, ten, or five,
　　To follow in a house where twice so many   170
　　Have a command t'attend you?
REGAN.   What need one?
LEAR.
　　Blood, fire! hear—Leprosies and bluest plagues!
　　Room, room for hell to belch her horrors up
　　And drench the Circes in a stream of fire!
　　Hark how th'Infernals echo to my rage   175
                              Lightning and thunder.

---

150. your] *Q1–2, 4–5;* you *Q3.*　　followers *Q2–3.*
152. what! fifty followers?] *Q4–5;*　　172. hear] *Q1;* here *Q2–5.*
what fifty followers *Q1;* what! fifty　　175. S.D.] *after l. 177 in Q1–5.*

Their whips and snakes—

REGAN.   How lewd a thing is passion!

GONERILL.

So old and stomachful.

LEAR.

Heavens drop your patience down;
You see me here, ye gods, a poor old man
As full of griefs as age, wretched in both—   180
I'll bear no more! No, you unnatural hags,
I will have such revenges on you both,
That all the world shall— I will do such things
What they are yet I know not, but they shall be
The terrors of the earth. You think I'll weep;

                                    Thunder again. 185

This heart shall break into a thousand pieces
Before I'll weep— O gods! I shall go mad.

                            Exit [followed by Kent].

DUKE.

'Tis a wild night, come out o'th'storm.   *Exeunt.*

                    End of the Second Act

175–76. *Infernals . . . snakes*] By the *Infernals* Lear means the snake-haired female furies who traditionally drive condemned souls through Hades.

176. *lewd*] ill-mannered.

177. *stomachful*] obstinate and self-willed.

ACT III

A desert heath.
                    Enter Lear *and* Kent *in the storm.*

LEAR.

    Blow, winds, and burst your cheeks; rage louder yet.
    Fantastic lightning singe, singe my white head.
    Spout cataracts, and hurricanos fall
    Till you have drowned the towns and palaces
    Of proud, ingrateful Man.   5

KENT.

    Not all my best entreaties can persuade him
    Into some needful shelter, or to 'bide
    This poor slight covering on his aged head,
    Exposed to this wild war of earth and heaven.

LEAR.

    Rumble thy fill, fight whirlwind, rain, and fire: 10
    Not fire, wind, rain, or thunder are my daughters.
    I tax not you, ye elements, with unkindness.
    I never gave you kingdoms, called you children,
    You owe me no obedience. Then let fall
    Your horrible pleasure; here I stand your slave,   15
    A poor, infirm, weak and despised old man.
    Yet I will call you servile ministers,
    That have with two pernicious daughters joined
    Their high-engendered battle against a head
    So old and white as mine. Oh! oh! 'tis foul.   20

KENT.

    Hard by, sir, is a hovel that will lend
    Some shelter from this tempest.

LEAR.

    I will forget my nature. What? so kind a father.
    Ay, there's the point.

KENT.

    Consider, good my liege, things that love night   25
    Love not such nights as this; these wrathful skies

---

17. I will] *Q1;* will I *Q2–5.*   24. Ay] *Q2–5;* I *Q1.*

2. *Fantastic*] unpredictable.
19. *high-engendered*] engendered in the heavens.

Frighten the very wanderers o'th'dark,
And make 'em keep their caves. Such drenching rain,
Such sheets of fire, such claps of horrid thunder,
Such groans of roaring winds have ne'er been known.   30

LEAR.

Let the great gods,
That keep this dreadful pudder o'er our heads
Find out their enemies now. Tremble thou wretch,
That hast within thee undiscovered crimes.
Hide, thou bloody hand,   35
Thou perjured villain, holy, holy hypocrite,
That drink'st the widow's tears, sigh now and cry
These dreadful summoners grace. I am a man
More sinned against than sinning.

KENT.

Good sir, to th'hovel.

LEAR.   My wit begins to burn.   40
Come on my boy, how dost my boy? Art cold?
I'm cold myself. Show me this straw, my fellow.
The art of our necessity is strange
And can make vile things precious. My poor knave,
Cold as I am at heart, I've one place there *Loud storm.* 45
That's sorry yet for thee.   *Exeunt.*

[III.ii]   *Gloster's palace.*
                           Enter Bastard.

BASTARD.

The storm is in our louder revelings drowned.
Thus would I reign could I but mount a throne.
The riots of these proud imperial sisters
Already have imposed the galling yoke
Of taxes and hard impositions on   5
The drudging peasants' neck, who bellow out

32. this] *Q1–2;* the *Q3–5.*
34. hast] *Q1, 5;* haste *Q2–4.*
35. thou] *Q1–2;* that *Q3–5.*
36. holy, holy] *Q1;* holy *Q2–5.*
42. me] *Q1–2; om. Q3–5.*

45. S.D. *Loud*] *Summers; Lond. Q1–5.*
46. S.D.*Exeunt*]*this edn.; Exit Q1–5.*

III.ii] *scene division not in Q1–5.*

32. *pudder*] turmoil.   42. *fellow*] fellow-sufferer.

Their loud complaints in vain. Triumphant queens!
With what assurance do they tread the crowd.
Oh for a taste of such majestic beauty,
Which none but my hot veins are fit t'engage!   10
Nor are my wishes desperate, for ev'n now
During the banquet I observed their glances
Shot thick at me; and as they left the room
Each cast by stealth a kind inviting smile,
The happy earnest—ha!   15

Two servants from several entrances deliver him each a letter, and exeunt.

(*Reads.*) "Where merit is so transparent, not to behold it
were blindness, and not to reward it ingratitude.
GONERILL."

Enough! blind and ingrateful should I be
Not to obey the summons of this oracle.   20
Now for a second letter.   *Opens the other* [*and reads*].
"If modesty be not your enemy, doubt not to find me
your friend.
REGAN."

Excellent sybil! O my glowing blood!   25
I am already sick of expectation,
And pant for the possession— Here Gloster comes
With business on his brow; be hushed, my joys.

[*Enter* Gloster.]

GLOSTER.

I come to seek thee, Edmund, to impart a business of
importance; I know thy loyal heart is touched to see the   30
cruelty of these ingrateful daughters against our royal
master.

BASTARD.

Most savage and unnatural.

GLOSTER.

This change in the state sits uneasy. The commons repine aloud at their female tyrants. Already they cry out   35

8. tread] *Q1;* treat *Q2–5.*   30. know] *this edn.;* knew *Q1–5.*

8. *tread*] oppress.
15. *earnest*] pledge.
20. *oracle*] an ironical comment on the ambiguity of Gonerill's note.
sybil (l. 25) continues the thought.

for the reinstallment of their good old king, whose injuries I fear will inflame 'em into mutiny.

BASTARD.

'Tis to be hoped, not feared.

GLOSTER.

Thou hast it boy, 'tis to be hoped indeed.
On me they cast their eyes, and hourly court me   40
To lead 'em on, and whilst this head is mine
I am theirs. A little covert craft, my boy,
And then for open action; 'twill be employment
Worthy such honest daring souls as thine.
Thou, Edmund, art my trusty emissary;   45
Haste on the spur at the first break of day
With these dispatches to the Duke of Cambrai.

                                        Gives him letters.

You know what mortal feuds have always flamed
Between this Duke of Cornwall's family and his.
Full twenty thousand mountaineers   50
Th'inveterate prince will send to our assistance.
Dispatch; commend us to His Grace, and prosper.

BASTARD *(aside)*.

Yes, credulous old man,
I will commend you to His Grace,
His Grace the Duke of Cornwall—instantly   55
To show him these contents in thy own character,
And sealed with thy own signet. Then forthwith
The choleric duke gives sentence on thy life;
And to my hand thy vast revenues fall
To glut my pleasure that till now has starved.   60

Gloster *going off is met by* Cordelia *entering* [*attended by* Arante];
Bastard *observing at a distance.*

CORDELIA.

Turn, Gloster, turn, by all the sacred powers
I do conjure you give my griefs a hearing.
You must, you shall, nay I am sure you will,
For you were always styled the just and good.

59. fall] *Q1–3; om. Q4–5.*   61. all] *Q1; om. Q2–5.*

47. *Cambrai*] Cambria, or Wales.   56. *character*] handwriting.
51. *inveterate*] full of obstinate hatred.

GLOSTER.

    What wouldst thou, princess? Rise and speak thy griefs. 65

CORDELIA.

    Nay, you shall promise to redress 'em too,
    Or here I'll kneel forever. I entreat
    Thy succor for a father and a king,
    An injured father and an injured king.

BASTARD.

    O charming sorrow! how her tears adorn her 70
    Like dew on flowers. But she is virtuous,
    And I must quench this hopeless fire i'th'kindling.

GLOSTER.

    Consider, princess,
    For whom thou begg'st, 'tis for the king that wronged thee.

CORDELIA.

    O name not that; he did not, could not wrong me. 75
    Nay muse not, Gloster, for it is too likely
    This injured king ere this is past your aid,
    And gone distracted with his savage wrongs.

BASTARD.

    I'll gaze no more—and yet my eyes are charmed.

CORDELIA.

    Or what if it be worse? Can there be worse? 80
    As 'tis too probable this furious night
    Has pierced his tender body, the bleak winds
    And cold rain chilled, or lightning struck him dead.
    If it be so, your promise is discharged,
    And I have only one poor boon to beg, 85
    That you'd convey me to his breathless trunk:
    With my torn robes to wrap his hoary head,
    With my torn hair to bind his hands and feet,
    Then, with a shower of tears,
    To wash his clay-smeared cheeks, and die beside him. 90

GLOSTER.

    Rise, fair Cordelia, thou has piety
    Enough t'atone for both thy sisters' crimes.
    I have already plotted to restore
    My injured master, and thy virtue tells me

---

80. Can ... worse?] *Q1; om. Q2–5.*

We shall succeed, and suddenly.   *Exit* [Gloster].
CORDELIA.   Dispatch, Arante,   95
    Provide me a disguise. We'll instantly
    Go seek the king, and bring him some relief.
ARANTE.
    How, madam? are you ignorant
    Of what your impious sisters have decreed?
    Immediate death for any that relieve him.   100
CORDELIA.
    I cannot dread the furies in this case.
ARANTE.
    In such a night as this? Consider, madam,
    For many miles about there's scarce a bush
    To shelter in.
CORDELIA.   Therefore no shelter for the king,
    And more our charity to find him out.   105
    What have not women dared for vicious love?
    And we'll be shining proofs that they can dare
    For piety as much. Blow winds, and lightnings fall:
    Bold in my virgin innocence, I'll fly
    My royal father to relieve, or die.
                Exeunt [Cordelia *and* Arante].   110
BASTARD.
    "Provide me a disguise, we'll instantly
    Go seek the king"—ha! ha! a lucky change.
    That virtue which I feared would be my hindrance
    Has proved the bond to my design.
    I'll bribe two ruffians that shall at a distance follow,   115
    And seize 'em in some desert place; and there
    Whilst one retains her t'other shall return
    T'inform me where she's lodged. I'll be disguised too.
    Whilst they are poaching for me I'll to the duke
    With these dispatches. Then to th'field,   120
    Where like the vig'rous Jove I will enjoy

---

110. S.D. *Exeunt*] *this edn.; Exit*   115. that] *Q1; om. Q2–5.*
Q1–5.   115. a] *Q1; om. Q2–5.*

    121–22. *Jove . . . storm*] In Ovid's *Metamorphoses* 3.5, Jove assumes mortal
form to woo Semele, herself mortal. She begs him to appear in all his
splendor as king of the gods, and when he does so she is destroyed by his
lightning and thunderbolts.

This Semele in a storm. 'Twill deaf her cries
Like drums in battle, lest her groans should pierce
My pitying ear, and make the amorous fight less fierce. *Exit.*

[III.iii]   *The field scene.*
                    Storm still. Enter Lear *and* Kent.

KENT.

Here is the place, my lord; good my lord, enter.
The tyranny of this open night's too rough
For nature to endure.   Let me alone.
LEAR.
KENT.

Good my lord, enter.
LEAR.   Wilt break my heart?
KENT.

Beseech you, sir.   5
LEAR.

Thou think'st 'tis much that this contentious storm
Invades us to the skin; so 'tis to thee;
But where the greater malady is fixed
The lesser is scarce felt: the tempest in my mind
Does from my senses take all feeling else   10
Save what beats there. Filial ingratitude!
Is it not as this mouth should tear this hand
For lifting food to't? But I'll punish home.
No, I will weep no more; in such a night
To shut me out— Pour on, I will endure   15
In such a night as this. O Regan, Gonerill,
Your old kind father whose frank heart gave all—
Oh, that way madness lies, let me shun that,
No more of that.
KENT.   See, my lord, here's the entrance.
LEAR.

Well, I'll go in   20
And pass it all. I'll pray, and then I'll sleep:
Poor naked wretches, wheresoe'er you are,

7. skin; so] *Q2–5;* skin so, *Q1.*   home *Q2–5.*
13. punish home] *Q1;* punish;   14. weep] *Q1; om. Q2–5.*

13. *punish home*] punish to the utmost.

44

That 'bide the pelting of this pitiless storm,
How shall your houseless heads and unfed sides
Sustain this shock? your raggedness defend you   25
From seasons such as these?
Oh, I have ta'en too little care of this.
Take physic, Pomp,
Expose thyself to feel what wretches feel,
That thou mayst cast the superflux to them   30
And show the heavens more just.

EDGAR *(in the hovel).*
Five fathom and a half! Poor Tom!

KENT.
What art thou dost grumble there i'th'straw?
Come forth.

[*Enter* Edgar, *disguised as a madman.*]

EDGAR.
Away! The foul fiend follows me—through the sharp   35
hawthorn blows the cold wind. Mum! go to thy bed and
warm thee.
(Aside.) Ha! what do I see?
By all by griefs, the poor old king bareheaded,
And drenched in this foul storm. Professing siren,   40
Are all your protestations come to this?

LEAR.
Tell me, fellow, didst thou give all to thy daughters?

EDGAR.
Who gives anything to poor Tom? whom the foul fiend
has led through fire and through flame, through bushes
and bogs, that has laid knives under his pillow, and   45
halters in his pew, that has made him proud of heart to
ride on a bay-trotting horse over four-inched bridges, to
course his own shadow for a traitor. —Bless thy five wits,
Tom's a-cold. *(Shivers.)* Bless thee from whirlwinds,

---

32. S.P. EDGAR . . . *hovel*] *Set be-*
tween ll. 31 and 32 as an entrance in
Q1–5.
36. thy] *Q1–3;* the *Q4–5.*

39. bareheaded] *Summers;* beheaded *Q1–5.*
40. foul] *this edn.;* fow *Q1–5.*

45–46. *laid . . . pew*] i.e., to tempt him into suicide.
48. *course*] chase.

star-blasting, and taking. Do poor Tom some charity,   50
whom the foul fiend vexes. —Sa, sa, there I could have
him now, and there, and there again.

LEAR.

Have his daughters brought him to this pass?
Couldst thou save nothing? Didst thou give 'em all?

KENT.

He has no daughters, sir.   55

LEAR.

Death, traitor, nothing could have subdued nature
To such a lowness but his unkind daughters.

EDGAR.

Pillicock sat upon Pillicock Hill; hallo, hallo, hallo.

LEAR.

Is it the fashion that discarded fathers
Should have such little mercy on their flesh?   60
Judicious punishment, 'twas this flesh begot
Those pelican daughters.

EDGAR.

Take heed of the foul fiend, obey thy parents, keep thy
word justly, swear not, commit not with man's sworn
spouse, set not thy sweet heart on proud array. Tom's   65
a-cold.

LEAR.

What hast thou been?

EDGAR.

A servingman proud of heart, that curled my hair,
used perfume and washes; that served the lust of my
mistress's heart, and did the act of darkness with her.   70
Swore as many oaths as I spoke words, and broke 'em all
in the sweet face of Heaven. Let not the paint, nor the
patch, nor the rushing of silks betray thy poor heart to
woman. Keep thy foot out of brothels, thy hand out of
plackets, thy pen from creditors' books, and defy the   75

61. this] *Q1–2;* his *Q3–5.*

---

50. *star-blasting*] blighting by an adverse star.

50. *taking*] bewitching.

62. *pelican*] Young pelicans traditionally feed on the life-blood of their
parent.

69. *washes*] liquid cosmetics.   73. *rushing*] rustling.

foul fiend—still through the hawthorn blows the cold
winds—sess, suum, mun, nonny, Dolphin my boy—hist!
the boy, sesey! soft, let him trot by.

LEAR.

Death! thou wert better in thy grave than thus to answer
with thy uncovered body this extremity of the sky. And   80
yet consider him well, and man's no more than this.
Thou art indebted to the worm for no silk, to the beast
for no hide, to the cat for no perfume—ha! here's two of
us are sophisticated. Thou art the thing itself; unac-
commodated man is no more than such a poor bare   85
forked animal as thou art.
Off, off, ye vain disguises, empty lendings.
I'll be my original self, quick, quick, uncase me.

KENT.

Defend his wits, good Heaven!

LEAR.

One point I had forgot; what's your name?   90

EDGAR.

Poor Tom, that eats the swimming frog, the walnut, and
the water-nut; that in the fury of his heart when the foul
fiend rages eats cow-dung for sallets, swallows the old rat
and the ditch-dog; that drinks the green mantle of the
standing pool; that's whipped from tithing to tithing;   95
that has three suits to his back, six shirts to his body,
Horse to ride, and weapon to wear,
But rats and mice, and such small deer
Have been Tom's food for seven long year.
Beware, my follower; peace, Smulkin; peace, thou foul   100
fiend.

LEAR.

One word more, but be sure true counsel; tell me, is a
madman a gentleman, or a yeoman?

78. the boy,] *Q1;* the boy! the boy!   accommated *Q1.*
Q2–3, 5; the boy the boy! *Q4.*   103. yeoman] *Q1, 3–5;* yeomen
85. unaccommodated] *Q2–5;* un-   *Q2.*

---

88. *uncase*] undress.
92. *water-nut*] a saligot, or water chestnut.
93. *sallets*] salads.
95. *from . . . tithing*] from one parish to another.

47

KENT.

 I feared 'twould come to this, his wits are gone.

EDGAR.

 Fraterreto calls me, and tells me Nero is an angler in the 105
 lake of darkness. Pray, innocent, and beware the foul
 fiend.

LEAR.

 Right, ha! ha! was it not pleasant to have a thousand with
 red hot spits come hizzing in upon 'em?

EDGAR *(aside)*.

 My tears begin to take his part so much   110
 They mar my counterfeiting.

LEAR.

 The little dogs and all, Trey, Blanch, and Sweetheart,
 see they bark at me.

EDGAR.

 Tom will throw his head at 'em; avaunt ye curs.
 Be thy mouth or black or white,   115
 Tooth that poisons if it bite,
 Mastiff, greyhound, mongrel grim
 Hound or spaniel, brach or hym,
 Bob-tail tight, or trundle-tail,
 Tom will make 'em weep and wail.   120
 For with throwing thus my head,
 Dogs leap the hatch, and all are fled.
 Ud, de, de, de. Se, se, se. Come march to wakes, and
 fairs, and market towns—Poor Tom, thy horn is dry.

LEAR.

 You sir, I entertain you for one of my hundred, only I 125
 do not like the fashion of your garments. You'll say
 they're Persian, but no matter, let 'em be changed.

Enter Gloster.

EDGAR.

 This is the foul Flibertigibet. He begins at curfew and

119. tight] *Q1;* Hight *Q2–5.*

---

105. *Fraterreto*] the name of a demon.
118. *brach*] a female hound.
118. *hym*] a lym or lymner, a species of bloodhound.

walks at first cock; he gives the web and the pin, knits the
elflock, squints the eye, and makes the harelip, mildews 130
the white wheat, and hurts the poor creature of the
earth;
Swithin footed thrice the cold,
He met the nightmare and her nine-fold,
   'Twas there he did appoint her;   135
He bid her alight and her troth plight,
   And aroint the witch, aroint her.

GLOSTER.

What, has Your Grace no better company?

EDGAR.

The Prince of Darkness is a gentleman; Modo he is
called, and Mahu.   140

GLOSTER.

Go with me, sir, hard by I have a tenant. My duty cannot
suffer me to obey in all your daughters' hard commands,
who have enjoined me to make fast my doors and let this
tyrannous night take hold upon you. Yet have I ven-
tured to come seek you out, and bring you where both 145
fire and food is ready.

KENT.

Good my lord, take his offer.

LEAR.

First let me talk with this philosopher.
Say, Stagirite, what is the cause of thunder?

GLOSTER.

Beseech you, sir, go with me.   150

LEAR.

I'll talk a word with this same learned Theban.
What is your study?

EDGAR.

How to prevent the fiend, and to kill vermin.

145. seek] *Q1–3;* to seek *Q4–5.*   151. talk] *Q1;* take *Q2–5.*

129. *walks at*] goes away.
129. *Web and the pin*] cataract of the eye.
130. *elflock*] a tangle in horse's hair, supposedly made by elves.
135. *appoint*] arrange to meet.
137. *aroint*] probably used here to mean "avoid."
141. *tenant*] probably the Old Man of IV.ii See IV.ii. 14–15.
149. *Stagirite*] philosopher; Aristotle was born at Stagira in Macedonia.

LEAR.

Let me ask you a word in private.

KENT.

His wits are quite unsettled; good sir, let's force him 155
hence.

GLOSTER.

Canst blame him? his daughters seek his death. This
bedlam but disturbs him the more. Fellow, be gone!

EDGAR.

Child Rowland to the dark tower came,
His word was still "Fie, fo, and fum,   160
I smell the bloud of a British man."—Oh, torture!

                                        Exit [Edgar].

GLOSTER.

Now, I pritheee, friend, let's take him in our arms, and
carry him where he shall meet both welcome and
protection. [*To* Lear.] Good sir, along with us.

LEAR.

You say right, let 'em anatomize Regan, see what breeds 165
about her heart. Is there any cause in nature for these
hard hearts?

KENT.

Beseech Your Grace.

LEAR.

Hist!—make no noise, make no noise—so, so; we'll to
supper i'th'morning.   *Exeunt.*   170

[III.iv]   [*The field.*]
                    Enter Cordelia *and* Arante.

ARANTE.

Dear madam, rest ye here, our search is vain.
Look, here's a shed; beseech ye, enter here.

CORDELIA.

Prithee go in thyself, seek thy own ease;
Where the mind's free, the body's delicate.
This tempest but diverts me from the thought   5
Of what would hurt me more.

165. see] *Q1–2; for Q3–5.*   III.iv.] *scene division not in Q1–5.*
                                     3. in] *Q1–2; om. Q3–5.*

Enter two Ruffians.

1 RUFFIAN.

    We have dogged 'em far enough, this place is private.
    I'll keep 'em prisoners here within this hovel
    Whilst you return and bring Lord Edmund hither.
    But help me first to house 'em.   10

2 RUFFIAN.

    Nothing but this dear devil   *Shows gold.*
    Should have drawn me through all this tempest;
    But to our work.

        They seize Cordelia *and* Arante, *who shriek out.*

    Soft, madam, we are friends; dispatch, I say!

CORDELIA.

    Help, murder, help! gods! some kind thunderbolt   15
    To strike me dead.

        Enter Edgar.

EDGAR.

    What cry was that? Ha, women seized by ruffians?
    Is this a place and time for villainy?
    Avaunt, ye bloodhounds.   *Drives 'em with his quarter-staff.*

BOTH.

    The devil, the devil!   *Run off.*   20

EDGAR.

    O speak, what are ye that appear to be
    O'th'tender sex, and yet unguarded wander
    Through the dead mazes of this dreadful night,
    Where (though at full) the clouded moon scarce darts
    Imperfect glimmerings.

CORDELIA.   First say what art thou.   25

    Our guardian angel, that wert pleased t'assume
    That horrid shape to fright the ravishers?
    We'll kneel to thee.

EDGAR [*aside*].   O my tumultuous blood!

---

7. dogged] *Q1, 3–5;* dodg'd *Q2.*   23. dead] *Q1;* dread *Q2–5.*
11. this dear] *Q1;* this, dear *Q2–5.*

---

   19. S.D. *quarter-staff*] a pole or club about six feet long. This is the *ballow*
of IV.iv.193.

By all my trembling veins, Cordelia's voice!
'Tis she herself! My senses sure conform   30
To my wild garb, and I am mad indeed.

CORDELIA.

Whate'er thou art, befriend a wretched virgin,
And, if thou canst, direct our weary search.

EDGAR.

Who relieves poor Tom, that sleeps on the nettle, with
the hedge-pig for his pillow?   35
Whilst Smug plied the bellows
She trucked with her fellows,
    The freckle-faced Mab
    Was a blouze and a drab,
Yet Swithin made Oberon jealous.—Oh! torture.   40

ARANTE.

Alack, madam, a poor wandering lunatic.

CORDELIA.

And yet his language seemed but now well tempered.
Speak, friend, to one more wretched than thyself,
And if thou hast one interval of sense,
Inform us if thou canst where we may find   45
A poor old man, who through this heath has strayed
The tedious night. Speak, sawest thou such a one?

EDGAR (aside).

The king, her father, whom she's come to seek
Through all the terrors of this night. O gods!
That such amazing piety, such tenderness,   50
Should yet to me be cruel!
[To Cordelia].   Yes, fair one, such a one was lately here,
And is conveyed by some that came to seek him
T'a neighb'ring cottage; but distinctly where,
I know not.

CORDELIA.   Blessings on 'em.   55

---

44. hast] *Q1–3;* haste *Q4–5.*

36–40. *Whilst . . . jealous*] a nonsense song. *Smug* could be a dog's name;
in fairy lore Queen Mab is supposed to have betrayed her consort Oberon
with a fairy knight; *Swithin* is probably mentioned as a link with Edgar's
earlier rhyme at III.iii. 137–41.
39. *blouze*] a ruddy, fat-faced wench (*OED*).
39. *drab*] a slut.

Let's find him out, Arante, for thou see'st   *Going off.*
We are in Heaven's protection.

EDGAR.   O Cordelia!

CORDELIA.

Ha!—Thou knowest my name.

EDGAR.

As you did once know Edgar's.

CORDELIA.   Edgar!

EDGAR.

The poor remains of Edgar: what your scorn   60
Has left him.

CORDELIA.   Do we wake, Arante?

EDGAR.

My father seeks my life, which I preserved
In hopes of some blest minute to oblige
Distressed Cordelia, and the gods have giv'n it;
That thought alone prevailed with me to take   65
This frantic dress, to make the earth my bed,
With these bare limbs all change of seasons 'bide,
Noon's scorching heat, and midnight's piercing cold;
To feed on offals, and to drink with herds,
To combat with the winds, and be the sport   70
Of clowns, or what's more wretched yet, their pity.

ARANTE.

Was ever tale so full of misery!

EDGAR.

But such a fall as this I grant was due
To my aspiring love, for 'twas presumptuous,
Though not presumptuously pursued;   75
For well you know I wore my flames concealed,
And silent as the lamps that burn in tombs,
Till you perceived my grief, with modest grace
Drew forth the secret, and then sealed my pardon.

CORDELIA.

You had your pardon, nor can you challenge more.   80

EDGAR.

What do I challenge more?

---

66. *frantic dress*] the clothing of a lunatic.
71. *clowns*] peasants.

Such vanity agrees not with these rags.
When in my prosperous state, rich Gloster's heir,
You silenced my pretenses, and enjoined me
To trouble you upon that theme no more,   85
Then what reception must love's language find
From these bare limbs and beggar's humble weeds?

CORDELIA.

Such as the voice of pardon to a wretch condemned;
Such as the shouts
Of succoring forces to a town besieged.   90

EDGAR.

Ah! what new method now of cruelty?

CORDELIA.

Come to my arms, thou dearest, best of men,
And take the kindest vows that e'er were spoke
By a protesting maid.

EDGAR .   Is't possible?

CORDELIA.

By the dear vital stream that bathes my heart,   95
These hallowed rags of thine, and naked virtue,
These abject tassels, these fantastic shreds
(Ridiculous even to the meanest clown)
To me are dearer than the richest pomp
Of purple monarchs.

EDGAR.   Generous charming maid,   100
The gods alone that made, can rate thy worth!
This most amazing excellence shall be
Fame's triumph, in succeeding ages, when
Thy bright example shall adorn the scene,
And teach the world perfection.

CORDELIA.   Cold and weary,   105
We'll rest a while, Arante, on that straw,
Then forward to find out the poor old king.

EDGAR.

Look, I have flint and steel, the implements

91. new] *Q1–3;* knew *Q4–5.*

84. *pretenses*] claims or protestations.
94. *protesting*] i.e., protesting, or vowing, love.
97. *fantastic*] grotesque.
104. *adorn the scene*] grace the stage.

Of wandering lunatics. I'll strike a light,
And make a fire beneath this shed to dry   110
Thy storm-drenched garments, ere thou lie to rest thee.
Then fierce and wakeful as th'Hesperian dragon,
I'll watch beside thee to protect thy sleep;
Meanwhile, the stars shall dart their kindest beams,
And angels visit my Cordelia's dreams.   *Exeunt.* 115

[III.v]   *Scene, [Gloster's] palace.*
Enter Cornwall, Regan, Bastard, *Servants*. Cornwall *with Gloster's*
letters.

DUKE.
    I will have my revenge ere I depart his house.
    Regan, see here, a plot upon our state;
    'Tis Gloster's character, that has betrayed
    His double trust of subject and of host.
REGAN.
    Then double be our vengeance; this confirms   5
    Th'intelligence that we but now received,
    That he has been this night to seek the king.
    But who, sir, was the kind discoverer?
DUKE.
    Our eagle, quick to spy, and fierce to seize,
    Our trusty Edmund.
REGAN.   'Twas a noble service.   10
    O Cornwall, take him to thy deepest trust,
    And wear him as a jewel at thy heart.
BASTARD.
    Think, sir, how hard a fortune I sustain,
    That makes me thus repent of serving you!   *Weeps.*
    O that this treason had not been, or I   15
    Not the discoverer.
DUKE.   Edmund, thou shalt find
    A father in our love, and from this minute

0.1. *Gloster's palace]The Palace Q1–5.*   6. but now] *this edn.;* now now *Q1;*
4. host] *Q2–5;* ost *Q1.*   now *Q2–5.*

---

112. *Hesperian dragon*] The dragon Ladon guarded the golden apples
which hung from trees in the garden of the Hesperides, daughters of the
god of the West.

We call thee Earl of Gloster. But there yet
Remains another justice to be done,
And that's to punish this discarded traitor.   20
But lest thy tender nature should relent
At his just sufferings, nor brook the sight,
We wish thee to withdraw.

REGAN (*to* Edmund *aside*).

The grotto, sir, within the lower grove,
Has privacy to suit a mourner's thought.   25

BASTARD.

And there I may expect a comforter,
Ha, madam?

REGAN.   What may happen, sir, I know not,
But 'twas a friend's advice.   *Exit* Bastard.

DUKE.

Bring in the traitor.

                Gloster *brought in*.

                Bind fast his arms.

GLOSTER.

What mean Your Graces?   30
You are my guests, pray do me no foul play.

DUKE.

Bind him, I say, hard, harder yet.

REGAN.

Now, traitor, thou shalt find—

DUKE.

Speak, rebel, where hast thou sent the king?
Whom spite of our decree thou saw'st last night.   35

GLOSTER.

I'm tied to th'stake, and I must stand the course.

REGAN.

Say where, and why thou hast concealed him.

GLOSTER.

Because I would not see thy cruel hands
Tear out his poor old eyes, nor thy fierce sister
Carve his anointed flesh; but I shall see   40

---

21. lest] *Q2–5;* least *Q1.*   36. I must] *Q1–2;* must *Q3–5.*

36. *tied . . . course*] In bear-baiting the bear was secured to a stake and
attacked by "courses" or relays of dogs.

The swift-winged vengeance overtake such children.

DUKE.

See't shalt thou never. Slaves, perform your work,
Out with those treacherous eyes. Dispatch, I say.
If thou see'st vengeance—

GLOSTER.

He that will think to live till he be old,   45
Give me some help— Oh, cruel! oh! ye gods!

They put out his eyes.

SERVANT.

Hold, hold, my lord, I bar your cruelty,
I cannot love your safety and give way
To such a barbarous practice.

DUKE.   Ha, my villain.

SERVANT.

I have been your servant from my infancy,   50
But better service have I never done you
Than with this boldness—

DUKE.   Take thy death, slave. [*Wounds him.*]

SERVANT.

Nay, then revenge whilst yet my blood is warm.   *Fight.*

REGAN.

Help here—are you not hurt, my lord?

GLOSTER.

Edmund, enkindle all the sparks of nature   55
To quit this horrid act.

REGAN.   Out, treacherous villain,
Thou call'st on him that hates thee. It was he
That broached thy treason, showed us thy dispatches;
There—read, and save the Cambrian prince a labor;
If thy eyes fail thee call for spectacles.   60

GLOSTER.

O my folly!
Then Edgar was abused; kind gods, forgive me that.

REGAN.

How is't, my lord?

42. shalt thou] *Q1;* thou shalt
Q2–5.

59. *Cambrian*] Welsh; see III.ii. 47 above.

DUKE.

Turn out that eyeless villain, let him smell
His way to Cambrai. Throw this slave upon a dunghill.   65
Regan, I bleed apace, give me your arm.   *Exeunt.*

GLOSTER.

All dark and comfortless!
Where are those various objects that but now
Employed my busy eyes? Where those eyes?
Dead are their piercing rays that lately shot   70
O'er flowery vales to distant sunny hills,
And drew with joy the vast horizon in.
These groping hands are now my only guides,
And feeling all my sight.
O misery! what words can sound my grief?   75
Shut from the living whilst among the living;
Dark as the grave amidst the bustling world.
At once from business and from pleasure barred;
No more to view the beauty of the spring,
Nor see the face of kindred, or of friend.   80
Yet still one way th'extremest fate affords,
And even the blind can find the way to death.
Must I then tamely die, and unrevenged?
So Lear may fall: no, with these bleeding rings
I will present me to the pitying crowd,   85
And with the rhetoric of these dropping veins
Enflame 'em to revenge their king and me.
Then when the glorious mischief is on wing,
This lumber from some precipice I'll throw,
And dash it on the ragged flint below;   90
Whence my freed soul to her bright sphere shall fly,
Through boundless orbs, eternal regions spy,
And, like the sun, be all one glorious eye.   *Exit.*

End of the Third Act

---

66. Regan] *set as a S.P. in Q1–5.*

---

75. *sound*] i.e., "proclaim" and "measure or show the depth of."
84. *rings*] sockets.
89. *lumber*] body.

ACT IV

[IV.i]   *A grotto.*
     Edmund *and* Regan *amorously seated, listening to music.*

BASTARD.

    Why were those beauties made another's right,
    Which none can prize like me? Charming queen,
    Take all my blooming youth, forever fold me
    In those soft arms, lull me in endless sleep,
    That I may dream of pleasures too transporting   5
    For life to bear.

REGAN.   Live, live, my Gloster,
    And feel no death but that of swooning joy.
    I yield thee blisses on no harder terms
    Than that thou continue to be happy.

BASTARD.

    This jealousy is yet more kind. Is't possible   10
    That I should wander from a paradise
    To feed on sickly weeds? Such sweets live here
    That constancy will be no virtue in me.
    (Aside.)   And yet must I forthwith go meet her sister,
    To whom I must protest as much.   15
    Suppose it be the same; why, best of all,
    And I have then my lesson ready conned.

REGAN.

    Wear this remembrance of me. I dare now *Gives him a ring.*
    Absent myself no longer from the duke,
    Whose wound grows dangerous—I hope mortal.   20

BASTARD.

    And let this happy image of your Gloster,
                     Pulling out a picture, drops a note.
    Lodge in that breast where all his treasure lies.
                                Exit [Bastard].

REGAN.

    To this brave youth a woman's blooming beauties

---

1. were] *Q1–3, 5;* where *Q4.*   8. thee] *Q1–2;* the *Q3–5.*
3. all] *Q1; om. Q2–5.*   17. ready] *Q1;* already *Q2–5.*

0.1. *grotto*] a picturesque cave or cavern, forming an agreeable retreat.
17. *And*] if.

Are due; my fool usurps my bed. What's here?
Confusion on my eyes.   *Reads.*   25
"Where merit is so transparent, not to behold it were
blindness and not to reward it, ingratitude.
                                        GONERILL."
Vexatious accident! Yet fortunate too,
My jealousy's confirmed, and I am taught   30
To cast for my defense—

                Enter an Officer.

Now, what mean those shouts? and what thy hasty entrance?
OFFICER.
A most surprising and a sudden change.
The peasants are all up in mutiny,
And only want a chief to lead 'em on   35
To storm your palace.
REGAN.   On what provocation?
OFFICER.
At last day's public festival, to which
The yeomen from all quarters had repaired,
Old Gloster, whom you late deprived of sight
(His veins yet streaming fresh), presents himself,   40
Proclaims your cruelty, and their oppression,
With the king's injuries; which so enraged 'em
That now that mutiny which long had crept
Takes wing, and threatens your best powers.
REGAN.
White-livered slave!   45
Our forces raised and led by valiant Edmund
Shall drive this monster of rebellion back
To her dark cell. Young Gloster's arm allays
The storm his father's feeble breath did raise.   *Exeunt.*

---

26. so] *Q1–3; om. Q4–5.*   49. S.D. *Exeunt.] this edn.; Exit*
32. what thy] *Q1–3;* that thy *Q4–5.*   *Q1–5.*
49. raise] *Q1, 3–5;* rise *Q2.*

---

31. *cast*] machinate.   37. *last day's*] yesterday's (*OED*).

[IV.ii]   *The field scene.*
                           Enter Edgar.

EDGAR.

 The lowest and most abject thing of fortune
 Stands still in hope, and is secure from fear.
 The lamentable change is from the best,
 The worst returns to better— Who comes here?

   Enter Gloster, *led by an* Old Man.

 My father poorly led! deprived of sight!   5
 The precious stones torn from their bleeding rings!
 Something I heard of this inhuman deed
 But disbelieved it, as an act too horrid
 For the hot hell of a cursed woman's fury;
 When will the measure of my woes be full?   10

GLOSTER.

 Revenge, thou art afoot, success attend thee.
 Well have I sold my eyes, if the event
 Prove happy for the injured king.

OLD MAN.

 O, my good lord, I have been your tenant and your
 father's tenant these fourscore years.   15

GLOSTER.

 Away, get thee away, good friend, be gone.
 Thy comforts can do me no good at all,
 Thee they may hurt.

OLD MAN.   You cannot see your way.

GLOSTER.

 I have no way, and therefore want no eyes;
 I stumbled when I saw. O dear son Edgar,   20
 The food of thy abused father's wrath,
 Might I but live to see thee in my touch,
 I'd say I had eyes again.

EDGAR.

 Alas, he's sensible that I was wronged;
 And should I own myself, his tender heart   25

11. afoot] *Q1;* on foot *Q2–5.*

_____

12. *event*] outcome.

Would break betwixt th'extremes of grief and joy.

OLD MAN.

How now, who's there?

EDGAR.

A charity for poor Tom. Play fair, and defy the foul fiend.
(Aside.) O gods! and must I still pursue this trade,
Trifling beneath such loads of misery?   30

OLD MAN.

'Tis poor mad Tom.

GLOSTER.

In the late storm I such a fellow saw,
Which made me think a man a worm.
Where is the lunatic?

OLD MAN.   Here, my lord.

GLOSTER.

Get thee now away, if for my sake   35
Thou wilt o'ertake us hence a mile or two
I'th'way toward Dover, do't for ancient love,
And bring some covering for this naked wretch,
Whom I'll intreat to lead me.

OLD MAN.   Alack, my lord, he's mad.

GLOSTER.

'Tis the time's plague when madmen lead the blind.   40
Do as I bid thee.

OLD MAN.

I'll bring him the best 'parrel that I have
Come on't what will.   *Exit.*

GLOSTER.   Sirrah, naked fellow.

EDGAR.

Poor Tom's a-cold—I cannot fool it longer,
And yet I must—bless thy sweet eyes, they bleed;   45
Believe't poor Tom even weeps his blind to see 'em.

GLOSTER.

Knowest thou the way to Dover?

EDGAR.

Both stile and gate, horseway and footpath. Poor Tom
has been scared out of his good wits; bless every true
man's son from the foul fiend.   50

---

28. *a charity*] alms.
44. *fool it*] play the madman.

GLOSTER.

Here, take this purse; that I am wretched
Makes thee the happier: Heaven deal so still.
Thus let the griping usurer's hoard be scattered.
So distribution shall undo excess,
And each man have enough. Dost thou know Dover?   55

EDGAR.

Ay, master.

GLOSTER.

There is a cliff, whose high and bending head
Looks dreadfully down on the roaring deep.
Bring me but to the very brink of it,
And I'll repair the poverty thou bear'st   60
With something rich about me. From that place
I shall no leading need.

EDGAR.

Give me thy arm: poor Tom shall guide thee.

GLOSTER.

Soft, for I hear the tread of passengers.

Enter Kent *and* Cordelia.

CORDELIA.

Ah me! your fear's too true, it was the king.   65
I spoke but now with some that met him
As mad as the vexed sea, singing aloud,
Crowned with rank fumiter and furrow weeds,
With berries, burdocks, violets, daisies, poppies,
And all the idle flowers that grow   70
In our sustaining corn. Conduct me to him
To prove my last endeavors to restore him,
And Heaven so prosper thee.

KENT.   I will, good lady.
Ha, Gloster here! Turn, poor dark man, and hear
A friend's condolement, who at sight of thine   75

---

52. the] *Q1–4; om. Q5.*   67. sea,] *Q1–3;* sea *Q4–5.*
57. There is] *Q1;* There's *Q2–5.* 72. To . . . him] *Q1–3; om. Q4–5.*

---

64. *passengers*] passers-by.
68. *fumiter*] fumitory, "an herb of a [bitter-tasting] quality" (Kersey).
69. *burdocks*] coarse, prickly weeds common on waste ground.
72. *prove*] test.

Forgets his own distress, thy old true Kent.

GLOSTER.

How, Kent? From whence returned?

KENT.

I have not since my banishment been absent,
But in disguise followed the abandoned king;
'Twas me thou saw'st with him in the late storm.   80

GLOSTER.

Let me embrace thee. Had I eyes I now
Should weep for joy, but let this trickling blood
Suffice instead of tears.

CORDELIA.   O misery!
To whom shall I complain, or in what language?
Forgive, O wretched man, the piety   85
That brought thee to this pass, 'twas I that caus'd it.
I cast me at thy feet, and beg of thee
To crush these weeping eyes to equal darkness,
If that will give thee any recompense.

EDGAR (aside).

Was ever season so distressed as this?   90

GLOSTER.

I think Cordelia's voice! Rise, pious princess,
And take a dark man's blessing.

CORDELIA.   O, my Edgar,
My virtue's now grown guilty, works the bane
Of those that do befriend me. Heaven forsakes me,
And when you look that way, it is but just   95
That you should hate me too.

EDGAR.

O waive this cutting speech, and spare to wound
A heart that's on the rack.

GLOSTER.

No longer cloud thee, Kent, in that disguise.
There's business for thee and of noblest weight.   100
Our injured country is at length in arms,
Urged by the king's inhuman wrongs and mine,
And only want a chief to lead 'em on.
That task be thine.

90. ever] *Q1–3;* every *Q4–5.*

EDGAR *(aside).*

    Brave Britons, then there's life in't yet.   105

KENT.

    Then have we one cast for our fortune yet.

    Come, princess, I'll bestow you with the king,

    Then on the spur to head these forces.

    Farewell, good Gloster, to our conduct trust.

GLOSTER.

    And be your cause as prosperous as 'tis just.   *Exeunt.* 110

[IV.iii]   *Gonerill's palace.*

    Enter Gonerill, [Gentleman,] *attendants.*

GONERILL.

    It was great ignorance, Gloster's eyes being out,

    To let him live; where he arrives he moves

    All hearts against us. Edmund I think is gone,

    In pity to his misery, to dispatch him.

GENTLEMAN.

    No, madam, he's returned on speedy summons   5

    Back to your sister.

GONERILL.   Ha! I like not that,

    Such speed must have the wings of love. Where's Albany?

GENTLEMAN.

    Madam, within, but never man so changed;

    I told him of the uproar of the peasants,

    He smiled at it; when I informed him   10

    Of Gloster's treason—

GONERILL.   Trouble him no further,

    It is his coward spirit. Back to our sister,

    Hasten her musters, and let her know

    I have giv'n the distaff into my husband's hands.

    That done, with special care deliver these dispatches   15

    In private to young Gloster.

        Enter a Messenger.

MESSENGER.

    O madam, most unseasonable news,

7. Albany?] *Q3–5;* Albany *Q1–2.*

---

106. *cast*] chance; a *cast* is a throw of dice.

The Duke of Cornwall's dead of his late wound,
Whose loss your sister has in part supplied,
Making brave Edmund general of her forces.   20
GONERILL [*aside.*]
One way I like this well;
But being widow, and my Gloster with her,
May blast the promised harvest of our love.
[*To the* Gentleman.]   A word more, sir: add speed to your
     journey,
And if you chance to meet with that blind traitor,   25
Preferment falls on him that cuts him off.   *Exeunt.*

[IV.iv]   *Field scene.*
           [*Enter*] Gloster *and* Edgar.

GLOSTER.
When shall we come to the top of that same hill?
EDGAR.
We climb it now, mark how we labor.
GLOSTER.
Methinks the ground is even.
EDGAR.
Horrible steep; hark, do you hear the sea?
GLOSTER.
No, truly.   5
EDGAR.
Why then your other senses grow imperfect
By your eyes' anguish.
GLOSTER.   So may it be indeed.
Methinks thy voice is altered, and thou speak'st
In better phrase and matter than thou didst.
EDGAR.
You are much deceived; in nothing am I altered   10
But in my garments.
GLOSTER.   Methinks y'are better spoken.

10. am I] *Q1–4;* I am *Q5.*

---

19. *supplied*] compensated for.
[IV.iv]
   0.1. *Field scene*] Repetition of the setting for IV.ii suggests that Edgar,
supposedly leading his father to Dover Cliff, has really brought him in a
circle.

EDGAR.
Come on, sir, here's the place: how fearful
And dizzy 'tis to cast one's eyes so low.
The crows and choughs that wing the midway air
Show scarce so big as beetles. Halfway down   15
Hangs one that gathers samphire, dreadful trade!
The fishermen that walk upon the beach
Appear like mice, and yon tall anchoring bark
Seems lessened to her cock, her cock a buoy
Almost too small for sight; the murmuring surge   20
Cannot be heard so high. I'll look no more,
Lest my brain turn, and the disorder make me
Tumble down headlong.
GLOSTER.   Set me where you stand.
EDGAR.
You are now within a foot of th'extreme verge.
For all beneath the moon I would not now   25
Leap forward.
GLOSTER.   Let go my hand.
Here, friend, is another purse, in it a jewel
Well worth a poor man's taking; get thee further,
Bid me farewell, and let me hear thee going.
EDGAR.
Fare you well sir.—That I do trifle thus   30
With this his despair is with design to cure it.
GLOSTER.
Thus, mighty gods, this world I do renounce,
And in your sight shake my afflictions off;
If I could bear 'em longer and not fall
To quarrel with your great opposeless wills,   35
My snuff and feebler part of nature should
Burn itself out. If Edgar live, oh bless him.
Now, fellow, fare thee well.
EDGAR.   Gone, sir! Farewell.

14. choughs] *Q1–4;* coughs *Q5.*   37. live] *Q1;* lived *Q2–5.*

14. *choughs*] jackdaws.
16. *samphire*] a rock-herb, gathered on cliffs for use in pickling.
19. *cock*] cock-boat, dinghy.
36. *snuff*] i.e., useless and expendable. A snuff is a burnt-out candle wick.

And yet I know not how conceit may rob
The treasury of life; had he been where he thought,   40
By this had thought been past. —Alive, or dead?
Hoa sir, friend; hear you, sir, speak—
Thus might he pass indeed—yet he revives.
What are you, sir?

GLOSTER.   Away, and let me die.

EDGAR.

Hadst thou been aught but gosmore, feathers, air,   45
Falling so many fathom down
Thou hadst shivered like an egg; but thou dost breathe,
Hast heavy substance, bleed'st not, speak'st, art sound;
Thy life's a miracle.

GLOSTER.   But have I fall'n or no?

EDGAR.

From the dread summit of this chalky bourn: 50
Look up a-height, the shrill-tuned lark so high
Cannot be seen, or heard. Do but look up.

GLOSTER.

Alack, I have no eyes.
Is wretchedness deprived that benefit
To end itself by death?

EDGAR.   Give me your arm.   55
Up so, how is't? Feel you your legs? you stand.

GLOSTER.

Too well, too well.

EDGAR.

Upon the crown o' the cliff, what thing was that
Which parted from you?

GLOSTER.   A poor unfortunate beggar.

EDGAR.

As I stood here below, methought his eyes   60
Were two full moons, wide nostrils breathing fire.

45. Hadst] *Q1–4;* Hast *Q5.*
45. gosmore,] *Q1;* gosmore *Q2–5.*
48. bleed'st not, speak'st, art sound;] *Q1;* bleedst? Not speak!

Art sound? *Q2–5.*
49. life's] *Q2–5;* live's *Q1.*
58. crown] *this edn.;* Crow *Q1–2;* Brow *Q3–5.*

39. *conceit*] imagination.
45. *gosmore*] gossamer.
50. *bourn*] i.e., the cliff, "bourn" or boundary of the sea or the land.

It was some fiend. Therefore, thou happy father,
Think that th'all-powerful gods, who make them honors
Of men's impossibilities, have preserved thee.

GLOSTER.

'Tis wonderful; henceforth I'll bear affliction   65
Till it expire. The goblin which you speak of,
I took it for a man; oft-times 'twould say,
"The fiend, the fiend"; he led me to that place.

EDGAR.

Bear free and patient thoughts—but who comes here?

Enter Lear, *a coronet of flowers on his head. Wreaths and garlands about
him.*

LEAR.

No, no, they cannot touch me for coining, I am the king   70
himself.

EDGAR.

O piercing sight!

LEAR.

Nature's above art in that respect. There's your press-
money. That fellow handles his bow like a cow-
keeper—draw me a clothier's yard. A mouse! a mouse!   75
peace, hoa—there's my gauntlet, I'll prove it on a giant
—bring up the brown bills—O well-flown bird—i'th'
white!—hewgh! give the word.

EDGAR.

Sweet marjoram.

LEAR.

Pass.   80

GLOSTER.

I know that voice.

67. it] *Q1–3; om. Q4–5.*

---

69. *free*] free from sorrow.
73–74. *press-money*] the sum paid to a recruit when he was "impressed"
or seized for the army.
74–75. *handles . . . cow-keeper*] i.e., uses his bow as if it were a stick for
driving cows.
75. *clothier's yard*] An arrow's length was that of a cloth-yard.
77. *brown bills*] halberds (painted to prevent rust).
78. *white*] the inner part of an archer's target.

LEAR.

Ha! Gonerill with a white beard! They flattered me like a
dog, and told me I had white hairs on my chin before the
black ones were there; to say "Ay" and "No" to every-
thing that I said; "Ay" and "No" too was no good divin-   85
ity. When the rain came once to wet me, and the winds to
make me chatter; when the thunder would not peace at
my bidding, there I found 'em, there I smelt 'em out. Go
to, they are not men of their words. They told me I was a
king; 'tis a lie, I am not ague-proof.   90

GLOSTER.

That voice I well remember, is't not the king's?

LEAR.

Ay, every inch a king! When I do stare
See how the subject quakes.
I pardon that man's life; what was the cause?
Adultery? Thou shalt not die. Die for adultery!   95
The wren goes to't, and the small gilded fly
Engenders in my sight: let copulation thrive,
For Gloster's bastard son was kinder to his father
Than were my daughters got i'th'lawful bed.
To't luxury, pell-mell, for I lack soldiers.   100

GLOSTER.

Not all my sorrows past so deep have touched me,
As these sad accents; sight were now a torment—

LEAR.

Behold that simp'ring lady, she that starts
At pleasure's name, and thinks her ear profaned
With the least wanton word; would you believe it?   105
The fitcher nor the pampered steed goes to't
With such a riotous appetite: down from the waist they
are centaurs, though women all above; but to the girdle
do the gods inherit, beneath is all the fiend's; there's hell,
there's darkness, the sulphurous unfathom'd—fie! fie! 110
pah!—an ounce of civet, good apothecary, to sweeten

89. to] *this edn.;* too *Q1–5.*   91. is't] *Q1;* it's *Q2–5.*

94. *cause*] charge, indictment.
106. *fitcher*] fitchew, or polecat.
111. *civet*] "a perfume like musk, made of the excrement of the civet-cat"
(Kersey).

my imagination—there's money for thee.

GLOSTER.

Let me kiss that hand.

LEAR.

Let me wipe it first; it smells of mortality.

GLOSTER.

Speak, sir; do you know me?   115

LEAR.

I remember thy eyes well enough; nay, do thy worst,
blind Cupid, I'll not love— Read me this challenge, mark
but the penning of it.

GLOSTER.

Were all the letters suns, I could not see.

EDGAR.

I would not take this from report. Wretched Cordelia, 120
What will thy virtue do when thou shalt find
This fresh affliction added to the tale
Of thy unparalleled griefs?

LEAR.

Read.

GLOSTER.

What! with this case of eyes?   125

LEAR.

O ho! are you there with me? No eyes in your head, and
no money in your purse? Yet you see how this world
goes.

GLOSTER.

I see it feelingly.

LEAR.

What? art mad? A man may see how this world goes with 130
no eyes. Look with thy ears, see how yon justice rails on
that simple thief; shake 'em together, and the first that
drops, be it thief or justice, is a villain. —Thou has seen
a farmer's dog bark at a beggar?

112. there's] *Q1–3, 5;* there *Q4.*   125. What!] *Q2–5;* What *Q1.*

120. *I would . . . report*] I would not believe this scene without witnessing
it.
122. *tale*] tally, sum.
125. *this case of eyes*] i.e., eyes in this state.

GLOSTER.

    Ay, sir.   135

LEAR.

    And the man ran from the cur; there thou might'st be-
    hold the great image of authority. A dog's obeyed in
    office. Thou rascal, beadle, hold thy bloody hand! Why
    dost thou lash that strumpet? Thou hotly lust'st to enjoy
    her in that kind for which thou whip'st her; do, do, the 140
    judge that sentenced her has been beforehand with thee.

GLOSTER.

    How stiff is my vile sense that yields not yet!

LEAR.

    I tell thee the usurer hangs the cozener; through tat-
    tered robes small vices do appear, robes and fur gowns
    hide all. Place sins with gold—why there 'tis for me, my 145
    friend, make much of it, it has the power to seal the
    accuser's lips. Get thee glass eyes, and, like a scurvy
    politician, seem to see the things thou dost not. Pull, pull
    off my boots; hard, harder, so, so.

GLOSTER.

    O matter and impertinency mixed!   150
    Reason in madness.

LEAR.

    If thou wilt weep my fortunes, take my eyes.
    I know thee well enough, thy name is Gloster.
    Thou must be patient, we came crying hither—
    Thou know'st, the first time that we taste the air   155
    We wail and cry—I'll preach to thee. Mark.

EDGAR.

    Break, lab'ring heart.

LEAR.

    When we are born, we cry that we are come
    To this great stage of fools.—

              Enter two or three Gentlemen.

GENTLEMAN.

    O! here he is; lay hand upon him. Sir,   160

135. Ay] *Q2–5;* I *Q1.*   160. him. Sir,] *this edn.;* him, Sir,
138. hold] *Q1;* hold up *Q2–5.*   *Q1;* him, Sir: *Q2–3;* him Sir: *Q4–5.*
154. came] *Q1;* come *Q2–5.*

Your dearest daughter sends—

LEAR.

No rescue? what, a prisoner? I am even the natural fool
of Fortune; use me well, you shall have ransom. Let me
have surgeons; oh I am cut to the brains.

GENTLEMAN.

You shall have anything.   165

LEAR.

No seconds? All myself? I will die bravely like a smug
bridegroom, flushed and pampered as a priest's whore. I
am a king, my masters, know ye that?

GENTLEMAN.

You are a royal one, and we obey you.

LEAR.

It were an excellent strategem to shoe a troop of horse 170
with felt. I'll put in proof—no noise, no noise—now will
we steal upon these sons-in-law, and then—kill, kill, kill,
kill!   *Exit running [pursued by* Gentlemen.]

GLOSTER.

A sight most moving in the meanest wretch,
Past speaking in a king. Now, good sir, what are you?   175

EDGAR.

A most poor man made tame to Fortune's strokes,
And prone to pity by experienced sorrows;
Give me your hand.

GLOSTER.

You ever-gentle gods, take my breath from me,
And let not my ill genius tempt me more   180
To die before you please.

                    Enter Gonerill's Gentleman-Usher.

GENTLEMAN.

A proclaimed prize! O most happily met,
That eyeless head of thine was first framed flesh
To raise my fortunes. Thou old unhappy traitor,
The sword is out that must destroy thee.   185

171. no noise,] *Q1–3;* on noise,
Q4–5.

---

170. *I'll put in proof*] i.e., I'll demonstrate. Lear now walks about the
stage as if to test the silence of felt soles.

GLOSTER.

    Now let thy friendly hand put strength enough to't.

GENTLEMAN.

    Wherefore, bold peasant,
    Dar'st thou support a published traitor? Hence,
    Lest I destroy thee too. Let go his arm.

EDGAR.

    'Chill not let go, zir, without vurther 'casion.   190

GENTLEMAN.

    Let go, slave, or thou diest!

EDGAR.

    Good gentleman go your gait, and let poor volk pass;
    and 'chu'd ha' bin zwaggered out of my life it would not
    a bin zo long as 'tis by a vortnight. —Nay, an' thou com'st
    near th'old man, I'ce try whether your costard or my   195
    ballow be th'harder.

GENTLEMAN.

    Out, dunghill.

EDGAR.

    'Chill pick your teeth, zir; come, no matter vor your
    voines.   *[They fight.]*

GENTLEMAN.

    Slave, thou hast slain me; oh untimely death!   200

EDGAR.

    I know thee well, a serviceable villain,
    As duteous to the vices of thy mistress
    As lust could wish.

GLOSTER.   What, is he dead?

EDGAR.

    Sit you, sir, and rest you.
    This is a letter carrier, and may have   205
    Some papers of intelligence that may stand

---

188. traitor? Hence] *Q3–5;*   195. I'ce] *Q1;* I'st *Q2–5.*
traytor, hence *Q1;* traitor hence   197. Out,] *Q1, 3–5;* Our *Q2.*
Q2.   198. vor your] *Q1; om. Q2–5.*

---

190. *'Chill*] I will. "Ich" is West of England dialect for "I."
192. *go your gait*] go your way.
193. *and 'chu'd*] if I could.
195. *I'ce*] I shall.   196. *ballow*] cudgel, or quarter-staff.
195. *costard*] head.   199. *voines*] foins, or thrusts.

Our party in good stead to know—what's here?
>*Takes a letter out of his pocket, opens, and reads.*

"To Edmund, Earl of Gloster.

Let our mutual loves be remembered. You have many
opportunities to cut him off. If he return the conqueror 210
then I am still a prisoner, and his bed my jail, from the
loathed warmth of which deliver me, and supply the
place for your labor.

>GONERILL."

A plot upon her husband's life,   215
And the exchange my brother! Here i'th'sands
I'll rake thee up, thou messenger of lust,
Grieved only that thou hadst no other deathsman.
In time and place convenient I'll produce
These letters to the sight of th'injured duke   220
As best may serve our purpose. Come, your hand.
Far off methinks I hear the beaten drum,
Come, sir, I will bestow you with a friend.   *Exeunt.*

[IV.v]   *A chamber.*

Lear *asleep on a couch*; Cordelia, [Physician,] *and* Attendants, *standing by him.*

CORDELIA.

His sleep is sound, and may have good effect
To cure his jarring senses, and repair
This breach of nature.

PHYSICIAN.

We have employed the utmost power of art,
And this deep rest will perfect our design.   5

CORDELIA.

O Regan, Gonerill, inhuman sisters,
Had he not been your father, these white hairs
Had challenged sure some pity. Was this a face
To be exposed against the jarring winds?
My enemy's dog, though he had bit me, should   10
Have stood that night against my fire. He wakes,
Speak to him.

---

211. jail] *Q2–5* (gaol); goal *Q1*.   216. sands] *Q2–5;* sands. *Q1*.

GENTLEMAN.   Madam, do you, 'tis fittest.

CORDELIA.

How does my royal lord? How fares Your Majesty?

LEAR.

You do me wrong to take me out o'th'grave.
Ha! is this too a world of cruelty?   15
I know my privilege, think not that I will
Be used still like a wretched mortal; no,
No more of that.

CORDELIA.   Speak to me, sir, who am I?

LEAR.

You are a soul in bliss, but I am bound
Upon a wheel of fire, which my own tears   20
Do scald like molten lead.

CORDELIA.   Sir, do you know me?

LEAR.

You are a spirit, I know, where did you die?

CORDELIA.

Still, still, far wide.

PHYSICIAN.

Madam, he's scarce awake; he'll soon grow more composed.

LEAR.

Where have I been? Where am I? Fair daylight!   25
I am mightily abused, I should ev'n die with pity
To see another thus. I will not swear
These are my hands.

CORDELIA.   O look upon me, sir,
And hold your hands in blessing o'er me; nay,
You must not kneel.

LEAR.   Pray do not mock me.   30
I am a very foolish, fond old man,
Fourscore and upward, and to deal plainly with you,
I fear I am not in my perfect mind.

CORDELIA.

Nay then, farewell to patience; witness for me
Ye mighty powers, I ne'er complained till now!   35

LEAR.

Methinks I should know you, and know this man,

17. still] *Q1; om. Q2–5.*

---

26. *abused*] deluded, deceived. Thus also in l. 53.

Yet I am doubtful, for I am mainly ignorant
What place this is, and all the skill I have
Remembers not these garments, nor do I know
Where I did sleep last night—pray do not mock me—
For, as I am a man, I think that lady
To be my child Cordelia.

CORDELIA.   O my dear, dear father!

LEAR.

Be your tears wet? Yes, faith; pray, do not weep.
I know I have given thee cause, and am so humbled
With crosses since, that I could ask   45
Forgiveness of thee were it possible
That thou couldst grant it, but I'm well assured
Thou canst not; therefore I do stand thy justice.
If thou hast poison for me I will drink it,
Bless thee, and die.   50

CORDELIA.

O pity, sir, a bleeding heart, and cease
This killing language.

LEAR.   Tell me, friends, where am I?

GENTLEMAN.

In your own kingdom, sir.

LEAR.   Do not abuse me.

GENTLEMAN.

Be comforted, good madam, for the violence
Of his distemper's past. We'll lead him in,   55
Nor trouble him, till he is better settled.
Will't please you, sir, walk into freer air?

LEAR.

You must bear with me, I am old and foolish.

                                        They lead him off.

CORDELIA.

The gods restore you—Hark, I hear afar
The beaten drum, old Kent's a man of's word.   60
Oh for an arm
Like the fierce Thunderer's, when th'earth-born sons

---

45. *crosses*] troubles.
48. *stand thy justice*] accept your verdict.
62–63. *Like ... heav'n*] Jupiter (the thunderer) was rebelled against by
some of the Titans, who are the "earth-born sons" of l. 62. He suppressed
the uprising with the aid of thunderbolts.

Stormed heav'n, to fight this injured father's battle.
That I could shift my sex, and dye me deep
In his opposer's blood. But as I may   65
With women's weapons, piety and prayers,
I'll aid his cause: You never-erring gods
Fight on his side, and thunder on his foes
Such tempest as his poor aged head sustained;
Your image suffers when a monarch bleeds.   70
'Tis your own cause, for that your succors bring,
Revenge yourselves, and right an injured king.   [*Exit.*]

End of the Fourth Act.

69. tempest] *Q1;* tempests *Q2–5.*

---

64. *shift*] change.

ACT V

Scene, a camp.
                    Enter Gonerill *and* Attendants.

GONERILL.

    Our sister's powers already are arrived,
    And she herself has promised to prevent
    The night with her approach. Have you provided
    The banquet I bespoke for her reception
    At my tent?
ATTENDANT.   So, please Your Grace, we have.   5
GONERILL.

    But thou, my poisoner, must prepare the bowl
    That crowns this banquet. When our mirth is high,
    The trumpets sounding and the flutes replying,
    Then is the time to give this fatal draught
    To this imperious sister. If then our arms succeed,   10
    Edmund, more dear than victory, is mine.
    But if defeat or death itself attend me,
    'Twill charm my ghost to think I've left behind me
    No happy rival. (*Trumpet.*) Hark, she comes.   *Exeunt.*

[*The same.*]
                    Enter Bastard *in his tent.*

BASTARD.

    To both these sisters have I sworn my love,
    Each jealous of the other as the stung
    Are of the adder. Neither can be held
    If both remain alive. Where shall I fix?
    Cornwall is dead, and Regan's empty bed   5
    Seems cast by Fortune for me, but already
    I have enjoyed her, and bright Gonerill
    With equal charms brings dear variety,

14. S.D. *Trumpet*] *set at end of line 13*   V.ii.] *scene division not in Q1–5.*
in Q1–5.   2. of the] *Q1–3, 5;* of the *Q4.*

---

    2. *prevent*] come before, outstrip.
[V.ii]
    2. *jealous*] mistrustful.
    6. *cast*] allotted.

And yet untasted beauty. I will use
Her husband's countenance for the battle, then   10
Usurp at once his bed and throne.

Enter Officers.

My trusty scouts, y'are well returned! Have ye descried
The strength and posture of the enemy?

OFFICER.

We have, and were surprised to find
The banished Kent returned, and at their head;   15
Your brother Edgar on the rear; old Gloster
(A moving spectacle) led through their ranks,
Whose powerful tongue, and more prevailing wrongs,
Have so enraged their rustic spirits that with
Th'approaching dawn we must expect their battle.   20

BASTARD.

You bring a welcome hearing. Each to his charge.
Line well your ranks and stand on your award,
Tonight repose you, and i'th'morn we'll give
The sun a sight that shall be worth his rising.   *Exeunt.*

[V.iii]   *Scene, a valley near the camp.*
                  Enter Edgar *and* Gloster.

EDGAR.

Here, sir, take you the shadow of this tree
For your good host; pray that the right may thrive.
If ever I return to you again
I'll bring you comfort.   *Exit.*

GLOSTER.   Thanks, friendly sir;
The fortune your good cause deserves betide you.   5

        An alarum, after which Gloster *speaks.*

The fight grows hot; the whole war's now at work,
And the gored battle bleeds in every vein
Whilst drums and trumpets drown loud slaughter's roar.
Where's Gloster now, that used to head the fray,

---

10. *countenance*] authority.
13. *posture*] strategic position.
21. *hearing*] report.
22. *Line . . . award*] Form up carefully, and stand your ground.

And scour the ranks where deadliest danger lay?   10
Here like a shepherd in a lonely shade,
Idle, unarmed, and list'ning to the fight.
Yet the disabled courser, maimed and blind,
When to his stall he hears the rattling war,
Foaming with rage tears up the battered ground,
And tugs for liberty.
No more of shelter, thou blind worm, but forth
To th'open field; the war may come this way
And crush thee into rest. Here lay thee down
And tear the earth, that work befits a mole.   20
O dark despair! When, Edgar, wilt thou come,
To pardon, and dismiss me to the grave!   *A retreat sounded.*
Hark! a retreat. The king has lost or won.

    Re-enter Edgar, *bloody.*

EDGAR.

 Away, old man, give me your hand, away!
 King Lear has lost, he and his daughter ta'en.   25
 And this, ye gods, is all that I can save
 Of this most precious wreck! Give me your hand.

GLOSTER.

 No farther, sir, a man may rot even here.

EDGAR.

 What? In ill thoughts again? Men must endure
 Their going hence even as their coming hither.   30

GLOSTER.

 And that's true too.   *Exeunt.*

[V.iv]   [*The field.*]
Flourish. Enter, in conquest, Albany, Gonerill, Regan, Bastard. Lear,
Kent, Cordelia *prisoners.*

ALBANY.

 It is enough to have conquered; cruelty
 Should ne'er survive the fight. Captain o'th'guards,
 Treat well your royal prisoners till you have

14. his] *Q1;* the *Q2–5.*   V.iv.] *scene division not in Q1–5.*
19. lay] *Q1;* lie *Q2–5.*

---

13. *courser*] charger.

    Our further orders, as you hold our pleasure.

GONERILL (*to the* Captain, *aside*).

    Hark, sir, not as you hold our husband's pleasure   5
    But as you hold your life, dispatch your prisoners.
    Our empire can have no sure settlement
    But in their death; the earth that covers them
    Binds fast our throne. Let me hear they are dead.

CAPTAIN.

    I shall obey your orders.   10

BASTARD.

    Sir, I approve it safest to pronounce
    Sentence of death upon this wretched king,
    Whose age has charms in it, his title more,
    To draw the commons once more to his side.
    'Twere best prevent—

ALBANY.   Sir, by your favor,   15
    I hold you but a subject of this war,
    Not as a brother.

REGAN.   That's as we list to grace him.
    Have you forgot that he did lead our powers?
    Bore the commission of our place and person?
    And that authority may well stand up   20
    And call itself your brother.

GONERILL.   Not so hot,
    In his own merits he exalts himself
    More than in your addition.

              Enter Edgar, *disguised*.

ALBANY.   What art thou?

EDGAR.

    Pardon me, sir, that I presume to stop
    A prince and conqueror. Yet ere you triumph,   25
    Give ear to what a stranger can deliver
    Of what concerns you more than triumph can.
    I do impeach your general there of treason,
    Lord Edmund, that usurps the name of Gloster,

---

5. S.D. *to ... aside*] *after l. 5 in Q1–5.*   25. ere] *this edn.;* e'er *Q1–5.*

---

  11. *approve*] recommend.
  23. *your addition*] the rank you have bestowed on him.
  25. *triumph*] celebrate victory.

Of foulest practice 'gainst your life and honor.   30
This charge is true, and, wretched though I seem,
I can produce a champion that will prove
In single combat what I do avouch,
If Edmund dares but trust his cause and sword.

BASTARD.

What will not Edmund dare! My lord, I beg
The favor that you'd instantly appoint
The place where I may meet this challenger,
Whom I will sacrifice to my wronged fame.
Remember, sir, that injured honor's nice
And cannot brook delay.   40

ALBANY.

Anon, before our tent, i'th'army's view,
There let the herald cry.

EDGAR.

I thank Your Highness in my champion's name.
He'll wait your trumpet's call.

ALBANY.   Lead.

Exeunt. Manent Lear, Kent, Cordelia, *guarded.*

LEAR.

O Kent, Cordelia!   45
You are the only pair that I e'er wrong'd,
And the just gods have made you witnesses
Of my disgrace, the very shame of Fortune;
To see me chained and shackled at these years!
Yet were you but spectators of my woes,   50
Not fellow-sufferers, all were well!

CORDELIA.

This language, sir, adds yet to our affliction.

LEAR.

Thou, Kent, didst head the troops that fought my battle,
Exposed thy life and fortunes for a master
That had (as I remember) banished thee.   55

KENT.

Pardon me, sir, that once I broke your orders;
Banished by you, I kept me here disguised

---

33. *avouch*] maintain.   39. *nice*] sensitive.
38. *fame*] reputation.

To watch your fortunes, and protect your person.
You know you entertained a rough blunt fellow,
One Cajus, and you thought he did you service.   60

LEAR.

My trusty Cajus, I have lost him too!   *Weeps.*
'Twas a rough honesty.

KENT.   I was that Cajus,
Disguised in that coarse dress to follow you.

LEAR.

My Cajus too! wert thou my trusty Cajus?
Enough, enough—   65

CORDELIA.

Ah me, he faints! his blood forsakes his cheek,
Help, Kent—

LEAR.   No, no, they shall not see us weep,
We'll see them rot first. Guards, lead away to prison.
Come, Kent, Cordelia come,
We two will sit alone, like birds i'th'cage.   70
Then thou dost ask me blessing, I'll kneel down
And ask of thee forgiveness. Thus we'll live,
And pray, and sing, and tell old tales, and laugh
At gilded butterflies; hear sycophants
Talk of court news. And we'll talk with them too: 75
Who loses, and who wins, who's in, who's out.
And take upon us the mystery of things
As if we were Heaven's spies.

CORDELIA.   Upon such sacrifices
 The gods themselves throw incense.

LEAR.   Have I caught ye?
He that parts us must bring a brand from Heaven.   80
Together we'll out-toil the spite of hell,
And die the wonders of the world. Away.   *Exeunt, guarded.*

[V.v]   [*The camp.*]

Flourish. Enter before the tents, Albany, Gonerill, Regan, [Bastard,]
Guards, and Attendants; Gonerill *speaking apart to the* Captain *of the
guards entering.*

76. in,] *Q1–4;* in, and *Q5.*

81. *out-toil*] exhaust.

GONERILL.

    Here's gold for thee. Thou knowest our late command
    Upon your prisoners' lives; about it straight, and at
    Our evening banquet let it raise our mirth
    To hear that they are dead.

CAPTAIN.

    I shall not fail your orders.   *Exit* [Captain].   5

      Albany, Gonerill, Regan *take their seats.*

ALBANY.

    Now, Gloster, trust to thy single virtue, for thy soldiers,
    All levied in my name, have in my name
    Took their discharge. Now let our trumpets speak,
    And, herald, read out this.   [*Trumpet.*]

HERALD (*reads.*)

    If any man of quality, within the lists of the army, will 10
    maintain upon Edmund, supposed Earl of Gloster, that
    he is a manifold traitor, let him appear by the third
    sound of the trumpet. He is bold in his defense. [*First
    trumpet.*] Again. [*Second trumpet.*] Again.
        [*Third trumpet.*] *Trumpet answers from within.*
          Enter Edgar, *armed.*

ALBANY.

    Lord Edgar!

BASTARD.   Ha! my brother!   15

    This is the only combatant that I could fear,
    For in my breast guilt duels on his side.
    But, Conscience, what have I to do with thee?
    Awe thou thy dull legitimate slaves, but I
    Was born a libertine, and so I keep me.   20

EDGAR.

    My noble prince, a word. Ere we engage
    Into Your Highness's hands I give this paper.
    It will the truth of my impeachment prove
    Whatever be my fortune in the fight.

ALBANY.

    We shall peruse it.   25

---

20. born a] *Q1;* a born *Q2–5.*   25. peruse] *Q1–4;* pursue *Q5.*

    6. *virtue*] valor.

EDGAR.

    Now, Edmund, draw thy sword,
    That if my speech has wronged a noble heart,
    Thy arm may do thee justice. Here i'th'presence
    Of this high prince, these queens, and this crowned list,
    I brand thee with the spotted name of traitor,   30
    False to thy gods, thy father, and thy brother,
    And what is more, thy friend: false to this prince.
    If then thou shar'st a spark of Gloster's virtue,
    Acquit thyself, or if thou shar'st his courage,
    Meet this defiance bravely.

BASTARD.   And dares Edgar,   35

    The beaten, routed Edgar, brave his conqueror?
    From all thy troops and thee I forced the field.
    Thou hast lost the general stake; and art thou now
    Come with thy petty single stock to play
    This after-game?

EDGAR.   Half-blooded man,   40

    Thy father's sin first, then his punishment;
    The dark and vicious place where he begot thee
    Cost him his eyes. From thy licentious mother
    Thous draw'st thy villainy; but for thy part
    Of Gloster's blood, I hold thee worth my sword.   45

BASTARD.

    Thou bear'st thee on thy mother's piety,
    Which I despise. Thy mother being chaste
    Thou art assured thou art but Gloster's son.
    But mine, disdaining constancy, leaves me
    To hope that I am sprung from nobler blood,   50
    And possibly a king might be my sire.
    But be my birth's uncertain chance as 'twill,
    Who 'twas that had the hit to father me
    I know not; 'tis enough that I am I.

---

51. possibly] *Q1–3;* possible *Q4–5.*

---

30. *spotted*] blemished, disreputable.
39. *stock*] stake, as in gambling.
40. *after-game*] a second game played in order to reverse or improve the issue of the first.
40. *Half-blooded man*] bastard.
46. *bear'st thee on*] take pride in.

Of this one thing I'm certain—that I have   55
A daring soul, and so have at thy heart.
Sound, trumpet.   *Fight*, Bastard *falls*.

GONERILL. REGAN.
    Save him, save him.

GONERILL.
    This was practice, Gloster.
    Thou won'st the field, and wast not bound to fight   60
    A vanquished enemy. Thou art not conquered
    But cozened and betrayed.

ALBANY.   Shut your mouth, lady,
    Or with this paper I shall stop it—hold, sir.
    Thou worse than any name, read thy own evil:
    No tearing, lady, I perceive you know it.   65

GONERILL.
    Say if I do, who shall arraign me for't?
    The laws are mine, not thine.

ALBANY.
    Most monstrous! Ha, thou know'st it too?

BASTARD.
    Ask me not what I know,
    I have not breath to answer idle questions.   70

ALBANY.
    I have resolved—(*To* Edgar.)   Your right, brave sir, has
    conquered.
    Along with me, I must consult your father.
                    Exeunt Albany *and* Edgar.

REGAN.
    Help every hand to save a noble life;
    My half o'th'kingdom for a man of skill
    To stop this precious stream.

BASTARD.   Away ye empirics,   75
    Torment me not with your vain offices;
    The sword has pierced too far. Legitimacy
    At last has got it.

REGAN.   The pride of nature dies.

---

68. too?] *Q2–5;* too. *Q1.*

59. *practice*] treachery.
75. *empirics*] quacks.

GONERILL.

Away, the minutes are too precious,
Disturb us not with thy impertinent sorrow.   80

REGAN.

Art thou my rival then professed?

GONERILL.

Why, was our love a secret? Could there be
Beauty like mine, and gallantry like his
And not a mutual love? Just Nature then
Had erred. Behold that copy of perfection,   85
That youth whose story will have no foul page
But where it says he stooped to Regan's arms,
Which yet was but compliance, not affection;
A charity to begging, ruined beauty!

REGAN.

Who begged when Gonerill writ that? Expose it,   90

Throws her a letter.

And let it be your army's mirth, as 'twas
This charming youth's and mine, when in the bower
He breathed the warmest ecstasies of love,
Then, panting on my breast, cried "Matchless Regan!
That Gonerill and thou should e'er be kin!"   95

GONERILL.

Die, Circe, for thy charms are at an end!
Expire before my face, and let me see
How well that boasted beauty will become
Congealing blood and death's convulsive pangs.
Die and be hushed, for at my tent last night   100
Thou drank'st thy bane, amidst thy reveling bowls.
Ha! dost thou smile? Is then thy death thy sport?
Or has the trusty potion made thee mad?

REGAN.

Thou com'st as short of me in thy revenge
As in my Gloster's love. My jealousy   105
Inspired me to prevent thy feeble malice
And poison thee at thy own banquet.

GONERILL.   Ha!

---

80. *impertinent*] trivial.

BASTARD.

    No more, my queens, of this untimely strife.
    You both deserved my love and both possessed it.
    Come, soldiers, bear me in; and let   110
    Your royal presence grace my last minutes.
    Now, Edgar, thy proud conquest I forgive.
    Who would not choose, like me, to yield his breath
    T'have rival queens contend for him in death?   *Exeunt.*

[V.vi]   *Scene, a Prison.*
    Lear *asleep, with his head on* Cordelia's *lap.*

CORDELIA.

    What toils, thou wretched king, hast thou endured
    To make thee draw, in chains, a sleep so sound?
    Thy better angel charm thy ravished mind
    With fancied freedom. Peace is used to lodge
    On cottage straw; thou hast the beggar's bed,   5
    Therefore shouldst have the beggar's careless thought.
    And now, my Edgar, I remember thee.
    What fate has seized thee in this general wreck
    I know not, but I know thou must be wretched
    Because Cordelia holds thee dear.   10
    O Gods! a sudden gloom o'erwhelms me, and the image
    Of death o'erspreads the place. Ha! who are these?

        Enter Captain *and* Officers *with cords.*

CAPTAIN.

    Now, sirs, dispatch, already you are paid
    In part, the best of your reward's to come.

LEAR.

    Charge, charge upon their flank, their last wing halts;   15
    Push, push the battle, and the day's our own.
    Their ranks are broke, down, down with Albany.
    Who holds my hands? O, thou deceiving sleep,
    I was this very minute on the chase;

---

109. deserved (deserv'd)] *Q1–4;*   17. down, down] *Q1–3;* down
deserve *Q5.*   *Q4–5.*

---

   108. *untimely*] unseasonable.   [V.vi]   2. *draw*] i.e., enjoy.

And now a prisoner here. What mean the slaves?   20
You will not murder me?

CORDELIA.   Help earth and heaven!
For your souls' sakes, dear sirs, and for the gods'.

OFFICER.
No tears, good lady, no pleading against gold and preferment. Come, sirs, make ready your cords.

CORDELIA.
You, sir, I'll seize,   25
You have a human form, and if no prayers
Can touch your soul to spare a poor king's life,
If there be anything that you hold dear,
By that I beg you to dispatch me first.

CAPTAIN.
Comply with her request, dispatch her first.   30

LEAR.
Off, hell-hounds, by the gods I charge you spare her!
'Tis my Cordelia, my true pious daughter.
No pity? Nay then, take an old man's vengeance.

Snatches a partisan, and strikes down two of them; the rest quit Cordelia,
and turn upon him. Enter Edgar *and* Albany [*with* Attendants.]

EDGAR.
Death! Hell! Ye vultures, hold your impious hands,
Or take a speedier death than you would give.   35

CAPTAIN.
By whose command?

EDGAR.   Behold the duke, your lord.

ALBANY.
Guards, seize those instruments of cruelty.

CORDELIA.
My Edgar, oh!

EDGAR.
My dear Cordelia! Lucky was the minute
Of our approach. The gods have weighed our sufferings; 40
W'are past the fire, and now must shine to ages.

GENTLEMAN.
Look here, my lord, see where the generous king

33.1. *partisan*] a long-handled spear.
42. *generous*] courageous.

Has slain two of 'em.

LEAR.   Did I not, fellow?
I've seen the day, with my good biting falchion
I could have made 'em skip. I am old now,   45
And these vile crosses spoil me. Out of breath!
Fie, oh! Quite out of breath and spent.

ALBANY.

Bring in old Kent; and, Edgar, guide you hither
Your father, whom you said was near.   *Exit* Edgar.
He may be an ear-witness at the least   50
Of our proceedings.

Kent *brought in here.*

LEAR.   Who are you?
My eyes are none o'th'best, I'll tell you straight.
Oh, Albany! Well, sir, we are your captives,
And you are come to see death pass upon us.
Why this delay? Or is't Your Highness' pleasure   55
To give us first the torture? Say ye so?
Why here's old Kent and I, as tough a pair
As e'er bore tyrant's stroke. But my Cordelia,
My poor Cordelia here, oh pity!

ALBANY.

Take off their chains. Thou injured majesty,   60
The wheel of Fortune now has made her circle,
And blessings yet stand 'twixt thy grave and thee.

LEAR.

Com'st thou, inhuman lord, to soothe us back
To a fool's paradise of hope, to make
Our doom more wretched? Go to, we are too well   65
Acquainted with misfortune to be gulled
With lying hope. No, we will hope no more.

ALBANY.

I have a tale t'unfold so full of wonder
As cannot meet an easy faith;
But by that royal injured head 'tis true.   70

KENT.

What would Your Highness?

65. Go to] *Q2–5;* Go too *Q1.*

---

44. *falchion*] a light, curved sword.

91

ALBANY.   Know, the noble Edgar
   Impeached Lord Edmund since the fight, of treason,
   And dared him for the proof to single combat,
   In which the gods confirmed his charge by conquest.
   I left ev'n now the traitor wounded mortally.   75
LEAR.
   And whither tends this story?
ALBANY.   Ere they fought
   Lord Edgar gave into my hands this paper,
   A blacker scrowl of treason, and of lust,
   Than can be found in the records of hell.
   There, sacred sir, behold the character   80
   Of Gonerill, the worst of daughters, but
   More vicious wife.
CORDELIA.
   Could there be yet addition to their guilt?
   What will not they that wrong a father do?
ALBANY.
   Since then my injuries, Lear, fall in with thine,   85
   I have resolved the same redress for both.
KENT.
   What says my lord?
CORDELIA.   Speak, for methought I heard
   The charming voice of a descending god.
ALBANY.
   The troops by Edmund raised, I have disbanded.
   Those that remain are under my command.   90
   What comfort may be brought to cheer your age
   And heal your savage wrongs, shall be applied;
   For to your majesty we do resign
   Your kingdom, save what part yourself conferred
   On us in marriage.
KENT.   Hear you that, my liege?   95
CORDELIA.
   Then there are gods, and virtue is their care.
LEAR.
   Is't possible?

76. Ere] *this edn.;* E'er *Q1–5.*   96. there] *Q1–2;* they *Q3–5.*

---

78. *scrowl*] scroll, list.
85. *fall in with*] match or coincide with (*OED* 90d).

Let the spheres stop their course, the sun make halt,
The winds be hushed, the seas and fountains rest;
All nature pause, and listen to the change.   100
Where is my Kent, my Cajus?

KENT.   Here, my liege.

LEAR.

Why I have news that will recall thy youth.
Ha! didst thou hear't, or did th'inspiring gods
Whisper to me alone? Old Lear shall be
A king again.   105

KENT.

The prince, that like a god has power, has said it.

LEAR.

Cordelia then shall be a queen, mark that:
Cordelia shall be queen. Winds, catch the sound
And bear it on your rosy wings to heaven.
Cordelia is a queen.   110

Re-enter Edgar *with* Gloster.

ALBANY.

Look, sir, where pious Edgar comes
Leading his eyeless father. O my liege!
His wondrous story will deserve your leisure:
What he has done and suffered for your sake,
What for the fair Cordelia's.   115

GLOSTER.

Where is my liege? Conduct me to his knees to hail
His second birth of empire. My dear Edgar
Has, with himself, revealed the king's blest restoration.

LEAR.

My poor dark Gloster.

GLOSTER.

O let me kiss that once more sceptered hand!   120

LEAR.

Hold, thou mistak'st the majesty, kneel here.
Cordelia has our power, Cordelia's queen.
Speak, is not that the noble suffering Edgar?

108. be] *Q1;* be a *Q2–5.*

GLOSTER.

    My pious son, more dear than my lost eyes.

LEAR.

    I wronged him too, but here's the fair amends.   125

EDGAR.

    Your leave, my liege, for an unwelcome message.
    Edmund (but that's a trifle) is expired.
    What more will touch you, your imperious daughters
    Gonerill and haughty Regan, both are dead,
    Each by the other poisoned at a banquet.   130
    This, dying, they confessed.

CORDELIA.

    O fatal period of ill-governed life!

LEAR.

    Ingrateful as they were, my heart feels yet
    A pang of nature for their wretched fall.
    But, Edgar, I defer thy joys too long.   135
    Thou served'st distressed Cordelia; take her crowned,
    Th'imperial grace fresh blooming on her brow.
    Nay, Gloster, thou hast here a father's right,
    Thy helping hand t'heap blessings on their heads.

KENT.

    Old Kent throws in his hearty wishes too.   140

EDGAR.

    The gods and you too largely recompense
    What I have done; the gift strikes merit dumb.

CORDELIA.

    Nor do I blush to own myself o'erpaid
    For all my sufferings past.

GLOSTER.

    Now, gentle gods, give Gloster his discharge.   145

LEAR.

    No, Gloster, thou hast business yet for life.
    Thou, Kent and I, retired to some cool cell,
    Will gently pass our short reserves of time
    In calm reflections on our fortunes past,
    Cheered with relation of the prosperous reign   150

139. heads] *Q2–5;* head *Q1.*   *Q4–5.*
147. cool] *Q1–2;* clo *Q3;* close

141. *largely*] liberally.

Of this celestial pair. Thus our remains
Shall in an even course of thought be passed;
Enjoy the present hour, nor fear the last.

EDGAR.

Our drooping country now erects her head,
Peace spreads her balmy wings, and Plenty blooms.   155
Divine Cordelia, all the gods can witness
How much thy love to empire I prefer!
Thy bright example shall convince the world
(Whatever storms of Fortune are decreed)
That truth and viture shall at last succeed.

Exeunt omnes. 160

FINIS

---

151. *remains*] the remainder of our days.

EPILOGUE

Spoken by Mrs. Barry

Inconstancy, the reigning sin o'th'age,
Will scarce endure true lovers on the stage;
You hardly ev'n in plays with such dispense,
And poets kill 'em in their own defense.
Yet one bold proof I was resolved to give,   5
That I could three hours' constancy outlive.
You fear, perhaps, whilst on the stage w'are made
Such saints, we shall indeed take up the trade;
Sometimes we threaten—but our virtue may
For truth I fear with your pit-valor weigh: 10
For (not to flatter either) I much doubt
When we are off the stage, and you are out,
We are not quite so coy, nor you so stout.
We talk of nunneries—but to be sincere
Whoever lives to see us cloistered there,   15
May hope to meet our critics at Tangier.
For shame give over this inglorious trade
Of worrying poets, and go maul th'Alcade.
Well—since y'are all for blustering in the pit
This play's reviver humbly does admit   20
Your abs'lute pow'r to damn his part of it;
But still so many master-touches shine
Of that vast hand that first laid this design,
That in great Shakespeare's right, he's bold to say
If you like nothing you have seen today   25
The play your judgment damns, not you the play.

Spoken by Mrs. Barry] Elizabeth Barry was especially adept at delivering epilogues, and only Ann Bracegirdle spoke more of them than she. This epilogue obviously depends for its effect upon the speaker's timing and audience rapport.

16. *May . . . Tangier*] i.e., the actresses are as likely to enter nunneries as the pit gallants are to go to Tangier. Tangier had belonged to England since 1662. In November 1679 the Moors put Tangier under a siege which lasted, with brief truces, until January 1681. When Tate's Epilogue was spoken, numerous reports of sharp fighting were coming in.

Alcade] i.e., Alcalde; Spanish for the governor or commander of a fortress.

Appendix A

Tate's Shakespearean Text

Having settled on *King Lear* as his first play for adaptation, Tate appears to have worked exclusively from the printed Shakespearean text. Though Tate's age believed that *King Lear* had a basis in historical fact, there is no evidence that Tate used Holinshed, Geoffrey of Monmouth, Milton, or any of the other histories available. A parallel between the happy ending of Tate's play and that of *The Chronicle History of King Leir* (published in 1605) is inconclusive in its implications, nor do certain verbal parallels in these two plays do more than intrigue the source-hunter. Here are the parallels, with the *Leir* readings first (from Sidney Lee's edition, 1909):

Leir   [to Cordelia]. Why how now minion, are you grown so
          proud?   (I.iii.86)
Lear   [to Cordelia]. Now, minion, I perceive. . . .   (I.i.118)

Goneril.   He hath most intolerably abused me . . . and made
            mutinies amongst the commons.   (III.iii.91–92)
Gloster.   The commons repine aloud at their female tyrants.
            Already they cry out for the reinstallment of
            their good old king, whose injures I fear will
            inflame 'em into mutiny.   (III.ii.34–37)

Perillus.   Cease, good my Lord, to aggravate my woes
            With these kind words, which cuts my heart in two.
                                        (IV.ii.13)
Edgar.   O waive this cutting speech . . . .   (IV.ii.97)

Cambria.   And make [Cordelia] an example to the world,
            For after-ages to admire her penance.   (V.ii.105–6)
Edgar [of Cordelia]. This most amazing excellence shall be
            Fame's triumph in succeeding ages, when

Thy bright example shall adorn the scene,
And teach the world perfection.　　(III.iv.102–5)
Edgar.　　Thy bright example shall convince the world . . . .
　　　　　　　　　　　　　　　　　　　　(V.vi.158)

Ragan.　　A shame on these white-liver'd slaves, say I. (V.v.13)
Regan.　　White-livered slave!　　　　　　　(IV.i.45)

It will be noticed that in the lines cited above there is no intervening Shakespearean reading. In addition, a murderer in *Leir* "Shews a bag of money" (IV.vii.238 S.D.) to justify his villainy; one of Cordelia's assailants in the *History* "Shows gold" (III.iv.11 S.D.). Cambria is a character in the old play, and in Tate's III.ii Gloster sends Edmund with letters to the "Duke of Cambrai."

In theory, Tate had six Shakespearean printings from which to work: three quartos (Q1, 1608; Q2, 1619; Q3, 1655) and three folios (F1, 1623; F2, 1632; F3, 1663–64). The fact that some Shakespearean passages which he used appear only in quartos and others only in folios proves that he had before him both quarto and folio versions, as is illustrated by the following list of readings from the collation of the *History* with Shakespeare's *King Lear*:[1]

Shakespearean Passages Used by Tate	*Provenance*
I.i.103	Qq.
I.i.162	Qq.
I.iv.218	Qq.
I.iv.329	Ff.
II.iv.21	Ff.
II.iv.96–97	Ff.
II.iv.101	Ff.
II.iv.138–43	Ff.
III.iv.17–18	Ff.
III.iv.27	Ff.
III.iv.37	Ff.
III.iv.51	Ff.
IV.vi.165–70	Ff.
IV.vi.186	Ff.
V.ii.11	Ff.
V.iii.117	Ff.

1. The Cambridge Shakespeare *King Lear*, ed. Wm. A. Wright (London, 1895), is the source of all my data on variant Shakespearean readings.

In this list it will be seen at a glance that the first three readings, all in Act I, are from a quarto source and all subsequent examples from a folio. A complete collation of Tate with the printed Shakespeare tends to bear out the notion that Tate composed Act I mainly from a Shakespearean quarto, consulting a folio source when puzzled by difficult readings, while for his subsequent acts he reversed this procedure. Why he should do this is easily explained. He chose to end his first act on the high point of Lear's curse, and only the Shakespearean folios offered a suitable line or two for getting Albany and Gonerill offstage and bringing the act to a close (Shakespeare's I.iv.336–38, Tate's I.ii.99–101). Tate also elected to begin his second act with the scene of Edgar's betrayal and flight. Those speeches in Shakespeare of which Tate makes use here are in prose in the quartos, in verse in the folios. It therefore seems likely that Tate, seeing that the lines which he wanted were in densely-printed prose in the quarto, simply stayed with the folio's verse, and thereafter used the folio as his main source. Even a brief comparison of a Shakespearean quarto *King Lear* with a folio will show how impractical it would be for anyone writing a verse adaptation of the play to make any substantial use of a quarto if he had access to a folio. Tate's change to the folio eliminated unnecessary trouble, and was made just at a point where the quarto was rendering the task difficult. Allardyce Nicoll suggests that Tate might have worked from some version of *King Lear* now lost, such as a manuscript promptbook,[2] but it is highly unlikely that a free-lance worker such as Tate could have had access to the Duke's Theater scripts or promptbooks.

Although it appears certain that Tate was a free-lance adaptor, he could not have tried to sell his *Lear* to the higher-bidding theater. The acting rights to almost the entire Shakespeare canon belonged to the heirs of Davenant and Killigrew, and the Duke's Theater "owned" *King Lear*. Every Shakespearean adaptation staged before the theatrical union of 1682 appeared at the theater which held the original play. Thus Tate would have adapted *King Lear* knowing that if it was not accepted for performance at Dorset Garden it would not be performed anywhere. He may have added the grotto and prison episodes (IV.i, V.vi) knowing that Dorset Garden could supply scenery for them.

2. *Dryden As an Adapter of Shakespeare* (London, 1922), pp. 5–6.

There is still the question of which quarto and folio Tate used. Hazelton Spencer believes that "as a rule the Restoration adaptor follows a single text which can usually . . . be readily identified," and that until after the publication of the Fourth Folio an adaptor's source is usually the latest pre-Wars quarto.[3] He accepts Rudolf Erzgraeber's conclusion that Tate's sources were Shakespeare's Q2 and F3.[4] But Erzgraeber admits that he had before him Tate's *King Lear* only in the form of a translation of the 1759 edition,[5] and some of the passages he cites in his chain of reasoning are not by Tate at all. An examination of more reliable parallel readings leads me to the opinion that Tate's quarto source was either Q2 or Q3 and that the folio which he used so extensively was probably F1.

3. *Shakespeare Improved* (Cambridge, Mass., 1927), p. 175.
4. Ibid., p. 273, n. 11.
5. *Nahum Tate's und George Colman's Bühnenbearbeitungen des Shakespear'schen "King Lear"* (Weimar, 1897), p. 8.

Appendix B

Chronology

Approximate years are indicated by*. Dates for plays are those on which they were first made public, either on stage or in print.

Political and Literary Events	*Life and Major Works of Tate*
1631 Death of Donne. John Dryden born.	
1633 Samuel Pepys born.	
1635 Sir George Etherege born.*	
1640 Aphra Behn born.*	
1641 William Wycherley born.*	
1642 First Civil War began (ended 1646). Theaters closed by Parliament. Thomas Shadwell born.*	
1648 Second Civil War. Nathaniel Lee born.	
1649 Execution of Charles I.	
1650 Jeremy Collier born.	
1651 Hobbes's *Leviathan* published.	
1652 First Dutch War began (ended 1654).	Nahum Tate born.

Thomas Otway born.

1656

D'Avenant's *THE SIEGE OF RHODES* performed at Rutland House.

1657

John Dennis born.

1658

Death of Oliver Cromwell.

D'Avenant's *THE CRUELTY OF THE SPANIARDS IN PERU* performed at the Cockpit.

1660

Restoration of Charles II.

Theatrical patents granted to Thomas Killigrew and Sir William D'Avenant, authorizing them to form, respectively, the King's and the Duke of York's Companies.

Pepys began his diary.

1661

Cowley's *THE CUTTER OF COLEMAN STREET*.

D'Avenant's *THE SIEGE OF RHODES* (expanded to two parts).

1662

Charter granted to the Royal Society.

1663

Dryden's *THE WILD GALLANT*.

Tuke's *THE ADVENTURES OF FIVE HOURS*.

1664

Sir John Vanbrugh born.

Dryden's *THE RIVAL LADIES*.

Dryden and Howard's *THE INDIAN QUEEN*.

Etherege's *THE COMICAL REVENGE*.

1665

Second Dutch War began (ended 1667).

Great Plague.
Dryden's *THE INDIAN EMPEROR.*
Orrery's *MUSTAPHA.*

1666
Fire of London.
Death of James Shirley.

1667
Jonathan Swift born.
Milton's *Paradise Lost* published.
Sprat's *The History of the Royal Society* published.
Dryden's *SECRET LOVE.*

1668
Death of D'Avenant.
Dryden made Poet Laureate.
Dryden's *An Essay of Dramatic Poesy* published.
Shadwell's *THE SULLEN LOVERS.*
Etherege's *SHE WOULD IF SHE COULD.*

1669
Pepys terminated his diary.
Susanna Centlivre born.

1670
William Congreve born.
Dryden's *THE CONQUEST OF GRANADA,* Part I.

1671
Dorset Garden Theatre (Duke's Company) opened.
Colley Cibber born.
Milton's *Paradise Regained* and *Samson Agonistes* published.
Dryden's *THE CONQUEST OF GRANADA,* Part II.
THE REHEARSAL, by the Duke of Buckingham and others.
Wycherley's *LOVE IN A WOOD.*

1672
Third Dutch War began (ended 1674).

Graduated from Trinity College, Dublin.

Joseph Addison born.
Richard Steele born.
Dyden's *MARRIAGE A LA MODE*.

1674
New Drury Lane Theatre (King's
Company) opened.
Death of Milton.
Nicholas Rowe born.
Thomas Rymer's *Reflections on
Aristotle's Treatise of Poesy* (transla-
tion of Rapin) published.

1675
Dryden's *AURENG-ZEBE*.
Wycherley's *THE COUNTRY
WIFE*.*

1676
Etherege's *THE MAN OF MODE*.
Otway's *DON CARLOS*.
Shadwell's *THE VIRTUOSO*.
Wycherley's *THE PLAIN DEALER*.

1677
Rymer's *Tragedies of the Last Age
Considered* published.
Behn's *THE ROVER*.
Dryden's *ALL FOR LOVE*.
Lee's *THE RIVAL QUEENS*.

Poems published.

1678
Popish Plot.
George Farquhar born.
Bunyan's *Pilgrim's Progress* (Part I)
published.

BRUTUS OF ALBA produced at
Dorset Garden.

1679
Exclusion Bill introduced.
Death of Thomas Hobbes.
Death of Roger Boyle, Earl of Or-
rery.
Charles Johnson born.

THE LOYAL GENERAL produced
at Dorset Garden.

1680
Death of Samuel Butler.
Death of John Wilmot, Earl Of
Rochester.

Contributed to *Ovid's Epistles,
Translated by Several Hands*.
THE HISTORY OF KING RICH-

Dryden's *THE SPANISH FRIAR.*
Lee's *LUCIUS JUNIUS BRUTUS.*
Otway's *THE ORPHAN.*

1681

Charles II dissolved Parliament at Oxford.
Dryden's *Absalom and Achitophel* published.

ARD THE SECOND produced at Drury Lane as *THE SICILIAN USURPER.*

THE HISTORY OF KING LEAR produced at Dorset Garden.
THE INGRATITUDE OF A COMMONWEALTH: OR THE FALL OF CAIUS MARTIUS CORIOLANUS produced at Drury Lane.

1682

The King's and the Duke of York's Companies merged into the United Company.
Dryden's *The Medal, MacFlecknoe,* and *Religio Laici* published.
Otway's *VENICE PRESERVED.*

The Second Part of Absalom and Achitophel.

1683

Rye House Plot.
Death of Thomas Killigrew.
Crowne's *CITY POLITIQUES.*

1684

A DUKE AND NO DUKE produced at Drury Lane.

1685

Death of Charles II; accession of James II.
Revocation of the Edict of Nantes.
The Duke of Monmouth's Rebellion.
Death of Otway.
John Gay born.
Crowne's *SIR COURTLY NICE.*
Dryden's *ALBION AND ALBANIUS.*

CUCKOLDS-HAVEN produced at Dorset Garden.
Poems (enlarged edition).

1687

Death of the Duke of Buckingham.
Dryden's *The Hind and the Panther* published.
Newton's *Principia* published.

THE ISLAND-PRINCESS produced at Drury Lane.

105

1688

The Revolution.

Alexander Pope born.

Shadwell's *THE SQUIRE OF ALSATIA*.

1689

The War of the League of Augsburg began (ended 1697).

Toleration Act.

Death of Aphra Behn.

Shadwell made Poet Laureate.

Dryden's *DON SEBASTIAN*.

Shadwell's *BURY FAIR*.

Libretto for Purcell's *DIDO AND AENEAS*.

1690

Battle of the Boyne.

Locke's *Two Treatises of Government* and *An Essay Concerning Human Understanding* published.

1691

Death of Etherege.*

Langbaine's *An Account of the English Dramatic Poets* published.

1692

Death of Lee.

Death of Shadwell.

Tate made Poet Laureate.

Appointed Poet Laureate (Rymer appointed Historiographer-Royal).

1693

George Lillo born.*

Rymer's *A Short View of Tragedy* published.

Congreve's *THE OLD BACHELOR*.

Essay on Farce (preface to Second Edition of *A DUKE AND NO DUKE*).

1694

Death of Queen Mary.

Southerne's *THE FATAL MARRIAGE*.

1695

Group of actors led by Thomas Betterton left Drury Lane and established a new company at Lincoln's Inn Fields.

Congreve's *LOVE FOR LOVE*.

Southerne's *OROONOKO*.

1696
Cibber's *LOVE'S LAST SHIFT.*
Vanbrugh's *THE RELAPSE.*

A New Version of the Psalms of David
(with Nicholas Brady).

1697
Treaty of Ryswick ended the War
of the League of Augsburg.
Charles Macklin born.
Congreve's *THE MOURNING
BRIDE.*
Vanbrugh's *THE PROVOKED
WIFE.*

1698
Collier controversy started with the
publication of *A Short View of the
Immorality and Profaneness of the English Stage.*

1699
Farquhar's *THE CONSTANT
COUPLE.*

1700
Death of Dryden.
Blackmore's *Satire against Wit*
published.
Congreve's *THE WAY OF THE
WORLD.*

1701
Act of Settlement.
War of the Spanish Succession
began (ended 1713).
Death of James II.
Rowe's *TAMERLANE.*
Steele's *THE FUNERAL.*

1702
Death of William III; accession of
Anne.
The Daily Courant began publica-
tion.
Cibber's *SHE WOULD AND SHE
WOULD NOT.*

Appointment as Historiographer-
Royal added to Tate's Laureate-
ship.

1703
Death of Samuel Pepys.
Rowe's *THE FAIR PENITENT.*

107

1704
Capture of Gibraltar; Battle of Blenheim.
Defoe's *The Review* began publication (1704–13).
Swift's *A Tale of a Tub* and *The Battle of the Books* published.
Cibber's *THE CARELESS HUSBAND*.

1705
Haymarket Theatre opened.
Steele's *THE TENDER HUSBAND*.

1706
Battle of Ramillies.
Farquhar's *THE RECRUITING OFFICER*.

1707
Union of Scotland and England.
Death of Farquhar.
Henry Fielding born.
Farquhar's *THE BEAUX' STRATAGEM*.

INJURED LOVE, "designed to be acted at Drury Lane" but not produced.

1708
Downes' *Roscius Anglicanus* published.

1709
Samuel Johnson born.
Rowe's edition of Shakespeare published.
The Tatler began publication (1709–1711).
Centlivre's *THE BUSY BODY*.

1711
Shaftesbury's *Characteristics* published.
The Spectator began publication (1711–1712).
Pope's *An Essay on Criticism* published.

1713
Treaty of Utrecht ended the War

of the Spanish Succession.
Addison's *CATO*.

1714
Death of Anne; accession of
George I.
Steele became Governor of Drury
Lane.
John Rich assumed management
of Lincoln's Inn Fields.
Centlivre's *THE WONDER: A
WOMAN KEEPS A SECRET*.
Rowe's *JANE SHORE*.

1715
Jacobite Rebellion.
Death of Tate.
Rowe made Poet Laureate.
Death of Wycherley.

Nicholas Rowe succeeded Tate as
Poet Laureate.
Death of Nahum Tate.

1716
Addison's *THE DRUMMER*.

1717
David Garrick born.
Cibber's *THE NON-JUROR*.
Gay, Pope, and Arbuthnot's
*THREE HOURS AFTER MAR-
RIAGE*.

1718
Death of Rowe.
Centlivre's *A BOLD STROKE FOR
A WIFE*.

1719
Death of Addison.
Defoe's *Robinson Crusoe* published.
Young's *BUSIRIS, KING OF
EGYPT*.

1720
South Sea Bubble.
Samuel Foote born.
Steele suspended from the Gover-
norship of Drury Lane (restored
1721).
Little Theatre in the Haymarket
opened.

Steele's *The Theatre* (periodical) published.

Hughes's *THE SIEGE OF DAMAS-CUS.*

1721

Walpole became first Minister.

1722

Steele's *THE CONSCIOUS LOV-ERS.*

1723

Death of Centlivre.

Death of D'Urfey.

1725

Pope's edition of Shakespeare published.

1726

Death of Jeremy Collier.

Death of Vanbrugh.

Law's *Unlawfulness of Stage Enter-tainments* published.

Swift's *Gulliver's Travels* published.

1727

Death of George I; accession of George II.

Death of Sir Isaac Newton.

Arthur Murphy born.

1728

Pope's *The Dunciad* (first version) published.

Cibber's *THE PROVOKED HUS-BAND* (expansion of Vanbrugh's fragment *A JOURNEY TO LONDON).*

Gay's *THE BEGGAR'S OPERA.*

1729

Goodman's Fields Theatre opened.

Death of Congreve.

Death of Steele.

Edmund Burke born.

1730

Cibber made Poet Laureate.

Oliver Goldsmith born.

Thomson's *The Seasons* published.
Fielding's *THE AUTHOR'S FARCE*.
Fielding's *TOM THUMB* (revised as *THE TRAGEDY OF TRAGE-DIES*, 1731).

1731
Death of Defoe.
Fielding's *THE GRUB-STREET OPERA*.
Lillo's *THE LONDON MERCHANT*.

1732
Covent Garden Theatre opened.
Death of Gay.
George Colman the elder born.
Fielding's *THE COVENT GARDEN TRAGEDY*.
Fielding's *THE MODERN HUS-BAND*.
Charles Johnson's *CAELIA*.

1733
Pope's *An Essay On Man* (Epistles I–III) published (Epistle IV, 1734).

1734
Death of Dennis.
The Prompter began publication (1734–1736).
Theobald's edition of Shakespeare published.
Fielding's *DON QUIXOTE IN ENGLAND*.

1736
Fielding led the "Great Mogul's Company of Comedians" at the Little Theatre in the Haymarket (1736–37).
Fielding's *PASQUIN*.
Lillo's *FATAL CURIOSITY*.

1737
The Stage Licensing Act.
Dodsley's *THE KING AND THE MILLER OF MANSFIELD*.
Fielding's *THE HISTORICAL RE-GISTER FOR 1736*.